CUT

HIBO WARDERE

CUT

One woman's
fight against
FGM
in Britain today

**SIMON &
SCHUSTER**

London · New York · Sydney · Toronto · New Delhi

A CBS COMPANY

First published in Great Britain by Simon & Schuster UK Ltd, 2016
A CBS COMPANY

1 3 5 7 9 10 8 6 4 2

Simon & Schuster UK Ltd
1st Floor
222 Gray's Inn Road
London WC1X 8HB

www.simonandschuster.co.uk

Simon & Schuster Australia, Sydney
Simon & Schuster India, New Delhi

A CIP catalogue record for this book
is available from the British Library

Trade paperback ISBN: 978-1-4711-5398-3
eBook ISBN: 978-1-4711-5398-3

Typeset in the UK by M Rules
Printed in the UK by CPI Group (UK) Ltd, Croydon, CR0 4YY

MIX
Paper from
responsible sources
FSC
www.fsc.org   FSC® C020471

Simon & Schuster UK Ltd are committed to sourcing paper
that is made from wood grown in sustainable forests and support the Forest
Stewardship Council, the leading international forest certification organisation.
Our books displaying the FSC logo are printed on FSC certified paper.

To my children

Contents

Prologue

The sky at the windows had turned from black to a midnight blue, as the sounds of a waking Mogadishu began filtering in through our curtains. The hungry bleating of the sheep and goats we kept tethered outside carried through the air, as the neighbours busied themselves with breakfast, clattering pots and pans as they fed families who, like us, slept fifteen to a villa; a hungry baby cried for milk after a long sleep, while the chickens clucked and scratched around in the dirt in the hope of finding one little grain left over from the day before. And, of course, there was the clockwork crow of the cockerel, puffing out his wings as he emerged from his own slumber and once again beating the imam in his minaret to his call to morning prayers. In the distance, the sound of engines stoked up, as the men set out to work or to mosque, after a breakfast cooked by their wives. And, further away, fishermen were getting ready to cast their lines out for another day in the Indian Ocean, determined to return with a bigger catch than yesterday, perhaps a fish so huge they wouldn't have to work for the rest of the week.

I had been roused from my sleep by the light touch of Hoyo's hand stroking my legs, her gentle voice calling to me in the darkness.

'Hibo,' my mother sang in a whisper. 'Hibo . . . Wake up.'

And now, my bones still heavy with slumber, my hand in hers, she led me from the bedroom I shared with my cousins. I could just make out the sleeping silhouettes of Fatima, Amina and Saida in their single beds, just feet from me but far away in their dreams. My cotton nightdress had offered little relief from the heat of the Somali night, and now it flapped around my ankles as Hoyo led me through our silent villa.

It was not yet 5am, too early for the sunlight to have begun its creep through our windows and across the floors, but the warmth of the previous day – and every day before that – permeated each brick of our home. We lived with the heat, we were blind to it; the nights were hot in Somalia, the days even hotter.

Slivers of light shone out from under the doors of the rooms we passed, muted sounds of my aunties shuffling behind them, readying themselves for another day of cooking and cleaning.

Except today was different.

Hoyo took me into the kitchen, where she'd lit the fire in the middle of the room and filled our tin bath. Slowly, she pulled my nightdress over my head and lifted me, still sleepy, into the warm water. She started to wash me, dipping the cloth into the water and rubbing it in the soap, then gently transferring the suds to my skin. Over and over she went, her touch much lighter than I'd ever known before. She sang softly, as she always did, folk songs that had soothed my ears as a baby, long before I'd understood any of the words.

'My pretty girl . . . The prettiest in the world to me . . .'

Every so often she'd pull me towards her to kiss my temples and tell me how much she loved me. As my mind slowly surfaced to full consciousness, it didn't occur to me to ask why I'd been woken at this hour or why I was having a bath this morning rather than at night; instead, I simply basked in the haze of tenderness.

'Today is going to be a big day, Hibo,' Hoyo said, planting a kiss on my soapy shoulders. 'You're going to be a brave girl, and I will be there with you. You'll never forget it. And I will be there the whole time.' I smiled to myself, sleepy and warm, as she pulled me in for another hug. 'I love you,' she said, kissing my face again and again.

If I had looked more closely at her face, would I have seen anxiety trace a path across it? Would I have noticed that her brown eyes twinkled less than usual this morning?

Finally, it was time to get out of the bath. Hoyo hooked her hands under my armpits, as she'd done a thousand times before, and lifted me out of the water, drying me as gently as she'd washed me. Yet when she was finished, she didn't dress me in any of the beautiful clothes that I'd been given at my party – not the red-and-yellow dress with matching shoes, or even the blue one – instead, she put me in rags, an old dress that must have belonged to one of my cousins years before and now didn't even look fit for playing

3

hopscotch in. She forgot to put any underwear on me too, but that didn't matter; once my cousins were awake, I'd rummage through the bedroom drawers for some cotton briefs.

'Now come over here and eat some breakfast, Hibo,' Hoyo said.

My eyes lit up at the sight of *anjero*. I watched as she poured the creamy batter into the pan, and how it bubbled and fizzed into sourdough pancakes over the flames of the fire. She fished one out with a flat knife – it was as big as a dinner plate – and doused it in more butter and sugar than she would ever let me put on myself.

'Come and eat,' she said, scooping me on to her lap, my long skinny legs dangling over the sides of each of hers. My little pot-belly still ached from all the wonderful food from the last two days, but I did as she said, because she was my Hoyo and pancakes were my favourite.

As I ate, she kissed the back of my neck, again telling me, 'Everything is going to be fine today', before placing me back down on my feet as she got up to make me another *anjero*. And another. By the third one even my eyes weren't so greedy, and my stomach groaned inwardly.

'If you love me you will eat this as well,' Hoyo said.

And I ate it because I did – I loved my mother more than anything else in the whole wide world.

Hoyo was clutching a kettle of water as we stepped out of the kitchen and into our yard. The ground had already been swept and covered in water to stop the dust from wafting up as the day wore on. This process would be repeated as the sun made its way through the sky east to west, to save the wind blowing the dirt back into the villa that Hoyo and my aunties would spend the morning cleaning.

The water had turned the ground into a deep-golden yellow, and the pink flowers that sprouted from it would soon be coaxed open by the rising sun. Outside of our compound, the smoke from neighbouring chimneys poured into the awakening sky, billowing light grey against the electric blue that was paling with the sun's ascent.

Hoyo took my hand and held it more firmly than I had ever known her to, and together with my auntie, the three of us walked to the far end of our garden. There the boundaries were hidden by three or four huge trees that provided shade for us children to play under in the afternoons after school. The long branches that reached down and tickled the earth now camouflaged the hut that I'd watched go up in my honour over the last two days. I had, of course, seen the same light-brown canvas erected in honour of my cousins so many times before – I was familiar with the sticks that Hoyo bought from the market and hammered into the orange earth, how she and my aunties bound them tightly together with twine that would hold fast for nearly a fortnight. But today it was me who was being led towards it.

'You be brave,' my mother said, as she gave my hand another squeeze in hers. 'I'm right here . . .'

I didn't think to ask what was going to happen in that hut, or why I needed to be brave. Why should I have worried when my mother was right there beside me? It had never occurred to me

5

that anything bad could happen to me under her care. So as we approached the hut, moving aside the long branches of the tree like a leafy curtain, I felt only anticipation and the lingering sweetness of the *anjero* on my lips.

Three women were waiting outside the hut for us. They weren't wearing brightly coloured dresses like the ladies who'd visited my party bearing gifts; they weren't wearing the same happy smiles. Instead, they were covered from head to toe in the dark *abaya*, with a long shawl providing extra coverage for their heads. The two younger ladies addressed me and my mother.

'*Salaam alaikum,*' they said.

'*Alaikum salaam.*'

'Are you Hibo?' one of them asked me, and she allowed her face to wrinkle into a slight smile as I nodded.

Without letting go of my hand, Hoyo guided me into the hut. It wasn't yet day and already the heat in there was stifling. The ground was covered with a black cloth that crinkled when I walked on it. To the left a straw mattress that had been made by my aunties lay on the ground, the yellow grass dyed in brilliant reds and blues, and a pattern woven through it. I had sat at their knees many times as they'd made these mattresses for my cousins to lie on in one of these very same huts, so I knew with only a glance how many hours had gone into creating this one just for me, and in that moment I felt very special.

There wasn't much room to sit or even stand alongside the mattress, and the hut was immediately crowded as the two other women and my auntie entered behind us with the third woman

I'd yet to see properly. She was older than the other two – perhaps sixty, maybe even older – her skin darker, and her face wrinkled with lines. I noticed her hands were rough and ashen, starved – no doubt – of the rich cream we rubbed into our own. Yet she strode in with some authority, not shuffling or hunched over like other women of her age.

When she finally spoke, it was not in a soft tone like the other two ladies who had greeted us at the doorway, but in a bark that instantly silenced everyone else.

'You,' she said, pointing to one of the ladies. 'Sit behind her with your legs open. Hold her in between.'

The grown-ups rearranged themselves in the tiny space to let her pass through, and as she sat down on the black cloth I took my place as I'd been instructed in front of her, facing forward. Hoyo, who was standing to my left, had let go of my hand, and my auntie, on my right, kept throwing me a tight yet brief smile. I looked to Hoyo, who was no longer smiling, then shuffled backwards until I felt my bottom nudge against the lady behind me. As soon as I did, I felt her arms clamp down on my own, holding me so tightly across my chest that I thought only of the *anjero* in my tummy that must have been squashed fast.

Panicked, I quickly turned to my left, to search my mother's face for reassurance, but there was none. Instead, she looked away from me.

'Hoyo?' I tried. She stared directly at the ground.

The old woman perched on a tiny stool in front of me, as my auntie and the other lady knelt down on either side. The old woman didn't look at me once – instead, she rearranged her headscarf and washed her hands with water from the kettle that Hoyo had brought with us from the kitchen. Underneath the forearms of the woman behind me, my heart was beating so wildly in my chest that she surely must have felt it, and yet she didn't relax her grip one bit, not even when I tried to wriggle.

The old woman busied herself, washing her hands with soap, then rinsing them slowly as if in some kind of ritual. The canvas above me was getting brighter, the sound of birds was starting to cut through the silence of the early day, and as I lay pinned down in this tiny hut, under the arms of a stranger, my heartbeat was pounding in my ears. I tried to remind myself what Hoyo had said, that I would be fine, that she would be there, but I didn't know what was happening. What were they going to do to me?

And what if I had known? Would I have even entered the hut? Would I have let go of my mother's hand before we'd even left the kitchen? Would I have run away, out of the compound, into the streets, and then to where? My safety was here, in this hut, with my mother . . . I didn't know then that she was about to betray me in the most cruel of ways. Instead, I searched the faces of the women I loved for something, anything, to tell me I was OK. But I saw nothing.

'You're going to hold her leg,' the woman – the 'cutter', I would later discover – barked at my auntie. To my left, the other lady grabbed one of my thighs, pulling on it so hard, I felt that my leg might pop clean out of its socket. My auntie took hold of my right leg, without any of the gentleness of touch I'd known from her my entire life.

Prologue

'Pull up her dress,' the cutter ordered the woman sitting behind me.

For a split second I felt the respite of her hands release from my torso, just long enough to catch my breath, and in that moment she pulled at the sides of my dress, yanking it over my bottom in one swift movement. Even if there had been enough time to try to escape, I doubt my legs would have worked anyway. Instead, I remained paralysed by fear.

'Hoyo?' I tried again. But she kept her gaze down. 'Hoyo?' This time with more urgency. Nothing. My racing heart threatened to steal what little voice I could muster from beneath this woman's grip.

I stared instead at the cutter sitting in front of me, searching her face for any trace of warmth. I watched as she slowly unzipped the leather bag that hung from a long strap around her neck and rested on her belly. As she did, I noticed the index finger and thumb on her right hand were each tipped with a long fingernail, longer than any I'd ever seen before, almost turning them into a pair of pincers. She dipped her gnarly hand into the leather bag and, as she did, the bag fell open to reveal dozens of razors. These weren't like the ones I'd seen in our bathroom, though, they weren't clean shiny silver razors. These were brown and rusty, and caked with dried blood.

As the old woman selected one and dipped it into the kettle of water, she glanced up at me just for a second. And then I saw them, those black eyes, within each iris was a terrifying cloudy circle of white. She looked like a monster.

I screamed.

But it was as if no one could hear my pleas at all.

1

Why Here? Why Now?

Twenty-three years ago, I sat down at my kitchen table with two books in front of me. One was a Somali–English dictionary, the other was a book about female circumcision.

I wasn't really sure what I was looking for; I didn't know what information I would find in there. I hadn't been living in London very long, and I didn't speak English at the time. But I knew this book had some relevance to me. I knew inside its pages I would somehow find what I was looking for. And so, night after night, once I'd put my baby down to sleep, I would lift my tired ankles, swollen from my second pregnancy, on to a chair and read.

It took me nine months to translate that book, pausing beside each English word to look up the Somali equivalent in the dictionary. Each sentence, each paragraph, each page coming to mean more and more to me as my knowledge of the English language grew.

And then I saw three letters that were somehow familiar: FGM. The dictionary told me they stood for 'female genital mutilation'. I was twenty-four, a mother of one, and yet this was the first time I had read about what had been done to me when I was six years old. I closed my eyes and remembered my maternity notes at the hospital, those same three letters written and boxed in thick Biro at the top of my files as I had my son. I had no idea at that point what they meant; no one had talked to me about what had happened.

I remembered, too, the look on the face of the first British doctor who had ever examined me down there when I'd just arrived in the country; the horror in her eyes, the colour that left her cheeks, the way she went to the sink and splashed her face with cold water in an attempt to compose herself. Now I knew why, because I'd read about the cruel practice myself, I'd seen pictures for the first time of how young girls are mutilated. And I understood in that moment that I was one of them.

I put both books down and sobbed into my hands, taking in the brutal details of everything I'd read. I felt the arms of my husband, Yusuf, around my shoulders. It was of some comfort, but it did little to take away the pain. Not only of what I lived with day to day – the discomfort, the recurrent infections, the pain of making love with my husband, the horror of childbirth – but there was something else now, too. The flashbacks that had haunted me my whole life suddenly came thicker and faster to my mind: the eyes

12

of the woman who had cut me; the heat of the hut where I'd been kept for two weeks, surviving on little food or water; the fact that my mother looked away the whole time I was pinned down and cut without warning.

These are images that I've had to learn to live with. These are the pictures that my mind scrambles to avoid each time I close my eyes. But the worst thing about it is that these scenes are not relegated to history, they are being played out every day for other girls – and this is happening in Britain. A country that has given me refuge, a country I thought was a million miles from the barbaric practices of my own homeland.

The World Health Organization (WHO) has declared FGM a global epidemic. Due to migration, there is not one country in the world where girls are not at risk of FGM. Worldwide, it is estimated that 3 million girls undergo the procedure every single year and 130 million women live with the effects of female circumcision. I am one of them.*

Until I read that book, I'd had no idea exactly what had happened to me as a child. All I knew was that I urinated differently after I'd been cut, that instead of rushing to the bathroom, in and out in less than a minute, chastised by my mother for forgetting to wash my hands, it now took up to fifteen minutes to empty my bladder. All I knew was that I lived in pain and discomfort every single day. And so I set out to learn more about what had been done to me. The journey has lasted more than twenty years, and continues to

* http://www.plan-uk.org/because-i-am-a-girl/female-genital-mutilation-fgm/

this day. It has taken me from that book on my kitchen table to this one you are holding in your hands now, via schools and police stations and hospitals, where I've worked to raise awareness of the situation. Because after I'd discovered what FGM was and that it was still happening to girls today, it became clear to me that this wasn't just my problem, that it was a complex and widespread issue everyone should be made aware of. And this is what inspired me to write and educate.

The WHO has declared a list of twenty-nine countries – across western, eastern and north-eastern Africa, and in parts of the Middle East and Asia – in which FGM is prevalent. It defines FGM as 'procedures that intentionally alter or cause injury to the female genital organs for non-medical reasons' and lists four different types*:

Type 1 – Clitoridectomy: partial or total removal of the clitoris (a small, sensitive and erectile part of the female genitals) and, in very rare cases, only the prepuce (the fold of skin surrounding the clitoris).

Type 2 – Excision: partial or total removal of the clitoris and the labia minora, with or without excision of the labia majora (the labia are 'the lips' that surround the vagina).

---

* The definitions of FGM and medicalisation were first adopted in the document 'Female genital mutilation: a joint WHO/UNICEF/UNFPA [World Health Organization/United Nations Children's Fund/United Nations Population Fund] statement (1)' published by WHO in 1997, and reaffirmed in 2008 by ten United Nations (UN) agencies in 'Eliminating female genital mutilation: an interagency statement (2)'.

Type 3 – Infibulation: narrowing of the vaginal opening through the creation of a covering seal. The seal is formed by cutting and repositioning the inner, or outer, labia, with or without removal of the clitoris.

Type 4 – Other: all other harmful procedures to the female genitalia for non-medical purposes, e.g. pricking, piercing, incising, scraping and cauterising the genital area.

I had Type 3 carried out on me – my clitoris and my inner and outer labia were removed and then the whole area was stitched up, leaving a narrowed hole which partially covered my vagina. Through this tiny hole I was expected to urinate and menstruate. With no urethra exposed, it meant that my urine had to travel down inside the area that had been covered with my own skin and slowly trickle out one drop at a time. It was no wonder I was constantly suffering from urinary tract infections. The skin that has been sewn together eventually fuses, and so what remains of 'normal' genitals can only be described as looking like what's between the legs of a Barbie doll. A complete blank where my sexual organs should be, and just one tiny hole where once my vagina was. It is, if you see even a sketch of it, a complete denial of womanhood. To this day, I still cannot look at an image of FGM without feeling – and often being – physically sick.

And this is a procedure carried out every single day on women and girls around the world, often without anaesthetic or painkillers, frequently by untrained villagers with little anatomical knowledge, and rarely in any kind of sterile environment. Is it any wonder, then, that girls die? From shock, or haemorrhaging, or subsequent infection.

As a child growing up in Somalia, I can remember many girls who were prepared for their *gudnin* – their circumcision – who I never saw again. Their devastated families called it *inshallah* – God's will. And yet FGM is not a religious practice; there is nothing about FGM in the Bible or the Koran. It is a nonsensical cultural tradition of maiming girls that has been practised for generations. It predates Christianity and Islam, its roots stretching as far back as ancient Egypt, and has survived for thousands of years despite the havoc it can wreak on the female body.

There is not an area of the world that has not, at one time or another, practised some form of female circumcision, including in the West. Until the middle of the last century – and particularly in Victorian times – clitoridectomies were seen in both Britain and the United States as a cure for excessive masturbation and even epilepsy. Victorian gynaecologist Isaac Baker Brown claimed that, after clitoridectomy, 'intractable women became happy wives; rebellious teenage girls settled back into the bosom of their families; and married women formerly averse to sexual duties became pregnant'.* It was thought that removing the clitoris would stem a female's sexual desire, that it would 'tame' her. And this – to some extent – is why the practice continues, worldwide, to this day.

In July 2014, a report released by City University London and Equality Now estimated that there are 137,000 women and girls

---

* http://www.msmagazine.com/oct00/makingthecut.html

living in the UK who are affected by FGM. The report went on to predict that there are 60,000 girls under the age of fifteen in Britain who are at risk of being mutilated.* That's tens of thousands of girls who could be exposed to this barbaric cultural practice, held down and cut against their will. Who could be maimed for life, or even lose their life to a tradition that should long ago have disappeared. These are girls that your children and mine go to school with, the girls they share a desk or playdates with. These are the babies in cots next to your baby's on the maternity unit. These are children who listen to the same pop music as your children. There is no difference between those girls and their classmates, except thankfully most of their classmates will not live in fear of their parents telling them that it is time for their rite of passage, that it is time to know what it is to be a woman.

In some cultures, to be a woman is to be condemned to a lifetime of pain. To be a woman means subjection to child abuse, to ensure that your 'virtue' remains intact, that your sexuality is controlled and that you are accepted by your community. Unfortunately, by chance, I was born into one of those cultures – just like 60,000 other girls in Britain.

FGM is a British problem. FGM is a global problem. But we can all play our part in making it stop.

* 'Prevalence of Female Genital Mutilation in England and Wales: National and local estimates', Alison Macfarlane, City University London/Equality Now, 2014.

2

Kintir

The dust was kicked up from the dry earth in huge swirls, blurring my vision as the particles drifted in front of my eyes. I coughed as the air, thick with dirt, caught in my throat; when the dust settled back down to the ground where I sat, they were still there, their faces hungry for their pound of flesh, which was my humiliation.

'Are you cut?' the first girl said.

I looked down and started picking at a stray blade of grass that had unfurled from the dry earth. I knew not to lie, so in resisting the temptation I instead said nothing. Then another girl spoke.

'Is the *kintir* still on you, Hibo?'

Despite everything that my mother had said, they weren't going to go away. They knew the answers, but they'd keep on and on until I confessed it. Finally, with the last bits of the dusty air sticking in my throat, I spoke: 'No, I'm not cut, my mother says I'm not ready.'

'Not ready?'

'I was cut when I was four!' one boasted.

'I was three!'

My eyes stayed focused on the earth, desperate to look anywhere but at their taunting expressions, anywhere but around this exposed school playground.

'You're not cut!'

'You still have your *kintir*!'

'You're dirty!'

'I am not dirty!' I said, leaping to my feet. 'My mother gives me a bath every day!'

It was pointless, though. The girls laughed and clapped, and jumped around. Another victim plucked from the crowd, another girl with *kintir* caught out.

'The *kintir* is dirty! Hibo is dirty!' And then they danced and skipped, great plumes of dust being swept up from the floor by their sandals. They sang and chanted and I rubbed my eyes, pretending it was the dust that had made them weep.

'My mum says I'm not ready to be cut,' I tried again.

'You're a coward,' they sang. 'Coward! Coward! Coward!'

'I am not,' I said, but my voice was barely audible over their collective taunts.

'Hibo is dirty! Don't play with Hibo!' And then other girls looked over from across the yard, and I shuffled back towards the classroom.

Kintir

Hoyo was wrong – these girls didn't stop when I ignored them. She'd told me that bullies get tired after a while, that they find a new victim. But that hadn't been my experience. Every day they were there; they'd hunt me out from some corner of the playground, intent on resuming their breaktime game. They watched with delight as my face crumpled, as I tried to defend myself, telling them that it said nothing in the Koran about removing the *kintir*, that it didn't make you dirty, whatever it actually was. But they just laughed and jeered and sang some more, my words falling on deaf ears. Life at school was a constant battle.

Between school and *madrasa* we'd go home for a nap in the shade, where we were grateful for the gentle breeze that slowly shifted our curtains back and forth, desperate for any respite from the 40-degree heat of the Somali sun. The streets were empty between midday and 4pm, the shops shut up while their owners took a break from the thick Mogadishu air; even dogs and cats searched for a shady spot under a tree, or any other shadow that was cast on the dry ground. By the afternoon it was cooler in the classrooms of the *madrasa*, where we studied the Koran for hours and hours.

There might have been respite from the heat, but the bullying was relentless. I'd go to pick up my Koran and as soon as my hand reached it the whispers would start.

'Don't touch the Koran, you're not cut,' they hissed. 'You can't touch it, you're not clean.'

The teacher seemed to be as oblivious to their words as he was to my tears. Had he heard? If he had, he didn't say anything.

21

CUT

As I trudged home from school that day, their insults ringing in my ears, I knew there was no escape from them. I'd seen the same happen to other girls; I knew now why some of them lied and said that they'd been cut when they hadn't. It was too late for me to do the same. Those girls knew now for sure, all their suspicions were confirmed; there was no chance another playtime would go by, or another lesson at *madrasa*, without them making comments or faces, or singing songs about me.

I wanted to be the same as them; or, if not the same, I wanted them not to even notice I was there. Why couldn't I disappear into the dust that they kicked up in my face? Why couldn't I stay at home instead of going to school? Or why couldn't I be cut? Was I a coward? Perhaps my mother was wrong and they were right after all?

When I got home that afternoon, Hoyo lifted me on to her lap and asked me what was wrong. It made a change from other days, when I'd come home with my knuckles red and bleeding after having them rapped with the fat, hard stick the teachers used on us when we couldn't answer a question in maths. Then I'd long for her to pull me into her arms, to cover the back of my hand in soft kisses, when instead she'd take off her shoe and chase me around the house until I told her what I'd done to offend the teacher. Any Somalian mother would do the same, such was the respect that our teachers commanded.

Today, though, it was the children who had hurt me, and so she pulled my skinny legs up into her lap and rocked me gently in her arms. Here I was safe, here I was in a place that I could trust. In Hoyo's arms, everything was OK.

'Tell me what's wrong, Hibo,' she whispered in my ear, planting light kisses on my cheeks.

'They say I'm dirty,' I cried. 'They tell the other girls not to play with me because I still have *kintir*.'

My mother was silent for a second, then I felt her warm, soft chest heave with a great big breath.

'What have I told you, Hibo? Their words can't hurt you. That's all they are, just words. Ignore them.'

My mother was my world – like most young children, much of life's pain and cruelty could be cured by five minutes on her lap, wrapped tight in her embrace. But not this.

'I can't ignore them, Hoyo,' I said, turning to look at her. 'They won't play with me – do you hear what they say? They say I'm not cut, that I'm dirty. That I'm a coward.'

'Let them talk, Hibo,' she said. 'They'll get bored eventually.'

She had said the same thing to me a thousand times, but today I noticed a tiredness in her voice. A sigh that told me she wanted them to stop, too, that she knew that ignoring them wasn't going to make them give up. My mother never grew tired of my questions, but I detected a profound weariness in the way she breathed out, expelling the air from deep in her chest.

As the youngest child of three my days were spent at my mother's ankles, feeling the waft of her skirt as I played on the floor at her feet, or listening – while pretending to look busy with a game – as she chattered with my aunties. I knew they didn't think my mother should allow me to sit beside them as they weaved, or sewed, or prepared food together; I knew they didn't want me to listen to their adult conversation. But time and again I heard my mother brush away their concerns, and gently reach down to place a hand on my shoulder instead. 'She's no bother there,' she would tell the other women.

I'd always shared everything with my mother, and from the moment I could remember speaking it seemed that I always had an endless list of questions for her. Mostly they were things like, 'Why is it women who do all the cooking and cleaning? Why don't women work? Who says they have to stay at home and look after their husband?' My mother's answers were invariably the same, a mock shock in her voice, a playful reprimand for questioning the role of women, a firm answer that I would do just as she and all women before us had – but always with a welcome ear to greet my next enquiry.

The conversations between my mother and my aunties were always the same: what to eat, what to clean next, and men. Yet growing up there were never any men around. We shared our villa with them, but the only time we saw them was at mealtimes, and even then they'd sit and eat together rather than with us. This was the way in Somalia in those days, or at least in our home. I never once saw my mother and father together alone; my father didn't play with me; the men went out to work or mosque, and the women stayed at home. The men ate together, talked together, smoked together, and the women looked after the children. Occasionally I might feel a passing hand ruffle my hair, or the arms of an uncle reach down to pull me up for a brief hug, but that was the extent of the male influence in our family life. We were brought up by women, we were fed by women, bathed by women, put to bed by women, and it was only at night when the midnight sky was spattered with stars that I would listen to the voices of my father and his brothers as they sat in our courtyard talking while I drifted off to sleep. My closest relationship had always been with my mother; she was who I confided in.

As I cried in her lap, I felt the top of my head wet from her own tears. I didn't want Hoyo to cry. Would it make her feel better if I was cut too? Was that the answer? Was it really my *kintir* that was causing all this sadness? If I didn't have my *kintir*, would everything be OK? Would Hoyo stop crying?

They said it's just a little cut. *Gudnin*, they called it. I didn't understand what it meant; I didn't really understand what a *kintir* was either, only that it wasn't meant to be there. The word in English is clitoris.

It seemed to me that *gudnin* must be a good thing, otherwise why would the girls in the playground boast so much that it had been done to them? I wanted to be just like they were; that's why I wanted to have the little cut too, so they would play with me again. I didn't know why Hoyo had made me wait so long for mine; the other girls in the playground made me feel like a baby when they said they were cut at three or four. My cousins always teased me that I was a baby – that even at six years old, Hoyo still tucked me up in bed and kissed me goodnight – but there was a big difference between their gentle leg-pulling and the cruel jibes of the girls at school. I could remember my cousins' *gudnin*, the parties and the presents. I wanted to have the same.

25

Finally I looked up and told her, 'I want to be cut too, Hoyo. Then they'll let me play again.'

She took a deep breath then, and her hands wiped the tears first from my cheeks and then from her own.

'Really?' she said, as she searched my face.

And I nodded, even though I wasn't sure what I'd asked for. But I knew it must be something good because suddenly her frown turned into a huge smile, and her eyes lit up, bright and sparkling.

'OK, then,' she said, kissing my forehead. 'Let's do it.'

Hoyo jumped out of her chair and began talking excitedly about all the plans for *gudnin*. She was naming all my favourite foods, she was wondering about presents, about the friends and relatives who would come to the house, fiddling with her headscarf at the thought of it all. And I was sure then that *gudnin* must be a good thing, if it had the power to make the girls in the playground stop being mean to me, if it made Hoyo as happy as she now appeared to be.

I remember going to sleep that night, under a light cotton sheet and a moon that seemed some evenings to blaze as brightly as the sun it had replaced. I heard the gentle hum of my mother and my aunties planning my party; I heard the rustle of packets of food, of flour, of sugar, and a clang of pots and pans as they pulled them apart from one another.

And as I drifted off I felt happy because soon I would be like the other girls. The preparations for my *gudnin* had begun and the bullying in the playground would end. Soon everything would be better again.

3

Gudnin

When I woke the following morning, Hoyo was busying herself in the kitchen again with my aunties. In turn they came and cupped my sleepy head in their hands, each with a broad smile stretched wide across their face. 'Wow! You are going to be *gudnin!*' they exclaimed, kissing me on both cheeks. 'What a big girl!'

Hoyo seemed to glide that day, a little dance in her feet each time someone turned up at our door, their arms heavy with food and presents. Family members continued to arrive, each auntie or cousin slipping off their shoes at the door and shuffling into our home in bare feet, their long, colourful dresses trailing as they went. I breathed in hard the smell of all kinds of *oounzi* which the women had perfumed themselves with for this special day, *my* special day, and soon it mingled with all the different scents that wafted around our villa.

The women cooked all day while I played outside with my cousins, an endless supply of tantalising treats streaming from the stove. 'Eat whatever you want,' Hoyo told me, her arms resting on my bony shoulders. 'No one will stop you today.'

'Anything?' I said, my eyes lighting up on behalf of my belly.

Hoyo nodded and laughed.

The benches were laden with plates of sugary *halwa*, all kinds of pasta and rice, sweet pieces of goat, camel and sheep – *odka* – and my favourite soft biscuits, *icun*. No table in Somalia is complete without banana, but today there was papaya and coconut, and fresh-squeezed glasses of passion fruit. The men came and went, leaving the women to their business, tapping the top of my head and mumbling *'mashallah'* – 'God has willed it' – between mouthfuls, on their way back to work or to prayer. I kept expecting to hear my older sister Hadsan chastising me each time I took something from the kitchen. Ten years older than me, she shared a room with my older cousins. Hadsan lived in another part of the house and now she was a teenager my mother had taught her to apply make-up. She was beautiful; her skin was much paler than mine and everyone who came to the house would comment on how pretty she was. My cousins and I were the little rascals, and Hadsan spent her days checking up on us, telling our mothers if she caught us stealing food from the kitchen, or leaving it uncovered for the flies to tiptoe across with their dirty feet. I wasn't close to my sister because of the age gap; in fact, I only really heard her voice when she was telling me off about something, but not on that day. For my *gudnin*, I could do nothing wrong. My older brother, Abdi, was eight then, and like my sister slept in another part of the house and sat with the men in the evening. We never mixed with the boys, not even our own brothers, although sometimes we ate alongside them as they gobbled hungry mouthfuls, shovelling the food in with their fingers, eager to get back to their game of football. That day, though, the boys were in their element as they ran into the villa to refuel on all the sweet treats laid out on the tables. Like the men, they didn't say anything about my *gudnin*, they just took the food. Mealtimes were when I would have the opportunity to see my father, not every day but on special occasions, and especially at Eid. I would sit alongside him, mesmerised by his long beard and particularly fascinated by the food that got stuck on to each wiry black part of it. He always looked like a kind man to me; he'd pat my head and say 'hello'. He wore a bright white *imama* turban and every time he sat beside me I'd stare at the dazzling whiteness of it, wondering how my mother kept it clean. That day he came in and out of the house with the other men, but unlike the women, none of them told me I was brave, or that I was about to become a big girl. They weren't wearing bright, happy smiles like the women; they just came for the food.

And there were presents that day, so many presents! Beautifully embroidered dresses, a red-and-yellow one with matching shoes, others in bright blues and greens and pinks. And they were all for me. And for Hoyo there were congratulations, which lit up her face as each new arrival rushed to say well done to her. More than a few commented that it was 'about time', to which she would dip her eyes to the floor and say that I was still so skinny for my age, and that she had needed time to fatten me up.

Today I was the star of the show. It was my head that everyone wanted to pat, my cheeks that everyone wanted to kiss, me who was going to be a big girl – me they told to be brave, as I rushed past their legs on the way back out to play in the yard. It was the happiest of days.

The following morning I was allowed to stay home with Hoyo while my cousins went off to school. Today she wanted me at her side. The food that we'd enjoyed the day before still sat heavy in my tummy, and yet Hoyo cooked up an enormous lunch for the remaining guests. 'Eat,' she insisted, spooning more on to my plate, which I ate with my fingers.

The house was quieter now; a calmness had descended after the exhilaration of the previous day's party. All we did was eat and pray, and then eat some more. I'd kneel beside my mother on the *sali* and copy her as she reached forward to the ground, whispering the *salat*. And I noticed an extra prayer was added that day: 'Hopefully, Allah, things will go right for Hibo.' I whispered the same words myself, not knowing what they might mean.

As the sun beat down hot rays on the terracotta tiles of our roof, we sat together indoors, the windows wide open and the curtains whispering at them. There we dozed until the sound of my cousins coming home from school woke us from our slumber, and then the celebrations continued. Hoyo was happy and my tummy was full to bursting, and I felt more loved than I ever had in my whole life.

4

Butchery

Terror ripped through my body in a shattering wave, as my lungs struggled under the weight of the arms that crushed them; as my legs were forced into excruciating angles; as the cutter gripped her dirty razor and flicked the skin between my legs as she muttered 'In the name of God almighty' through her tight thin lips; as my mother turned her face away from me.

And that was more frightening than anything else – the fact that this person, who had bathed me so gently just moments ago, was abandoning me now, when I needed her the most.

'Hoyo!' I screamed again. 'Hoyo, Hoyo, HOYO!'

But even if she had moved now, opened her mouth to speak, to save me, to tell them to stop, it was already too late by then. Everything was underway.

'Open her legs wider,' the cutter ordered the women who were holding my legs. Then, with those long pincer nails, she dug between my legs and grasped my clitoris, my *kintir*. She pulled on it until it burned and for a second, as my eyes widened in horror, I thought she was going to pull it clean from my body with her fingers, or at least that those sharp nails might rip their way through my delicate skin.

But she had something far worse planned.

She lifted up that dirty razor, the one that still had the dried brown residue of others' blood clinging to it, like filthy reminders of her previous work, and she cut straight through my flesh.

The pain shot through me like a bullet. I felt as if someone had taken me and dropped me into bright-orange molten lava. From head to toe the pain burned, searing the backs of my eyes and exploding in my brain.

I screamed then. An almost inhuman scream, a sound I hadn't known I was capable of making.

'Hoyo!' I cried, as I tried to shake her, wake her, make her hear my pleas. She didn't flinch; instead, she reached for her scarf and gathered more of it up under her chin, as if to protect herself from the horror. Her ears, beneath that *hijab*, deaf to my screams.

It was the cutter's cold voice I heard in reply.

'There's still some left,' she said.

And she cut again, and again, and again.

With each slice of her razor she took more and more of my flesh. There was no time for my brain to process what was happening between my legs. I was a piece of meat on a butcher's board that the cutter was trimming bits of fat off. I was not a child, not a soul, not a six-year-old begging for help.

She picked up a cloth and dabbed it between my legs; each time she took it away, I saw that more and more of it was soaked in red. I could smell my blood by now, the sickly metal tang of it filling the small hut that we were crammed into. The pain continued, each hack into my flesh seeming to hit a new place and every nerve ending screaming in agony.

I knew in that moment that this wasn't humane, to make me suffer like this; we would never have let one of our animals suffer in this way, we would put even a goat or a sheep out of its misery sooner than let it experience this pain. On and on it went, and then further, as she parted my vaginal lips and hacked away at more flesh inside. Everything was on fire, and all I could do was scream.

Finally, the cutter snapped. 'I can't concentrate!' she barked at my mother. 'She is making too much noise. I've done many, many girls, none of them screamed like her. What's wrong with her? Get her to be quiet!'

It was then, for the first time since we entered the hut, that Hoyo spoke. Not in response to her daughter's pitiful cries, but in collusion with the cutter who was torturing her youngest child.

'Hibo, stop screaming!' she said quickly. 'The girls will hear you, you will be called a coward. Stop screaming.'

Her words hurt more than anything this cutter was doing to me. Her betrayal was absolute.

I was drowning in a raging river of pain and I couldn't swim free. I didn't want to drown, I wouldn't drown! I would stay afloat, and the only way I could do that was to allow it to take me. And so I surrendered to the cutter, I surrendered to the pain.

After she finished slicing at my inner labia, she then moved on to my outer ones. The sounds that were coming from me now were involuntary, subconscious, a whimpering, a keening that I had no control over.

The cutter hacked away, my mother watched on, my auntie held me down.

By the time the cutter put down her razor my body had taken over. I was shaking so much with shock, my teeth chattering – shivering even in 36-degree heat. I opened my eyes for a moment, thinking at last the attack had come to an end. Instead the cutter said, 'Hold her tight, this is the important bit.'

Through eyes blurred with tears I saw an acacia thorn in her hand, and into it she was weaving a thick thread. This thorn was not fine like the needles I saw my mother making our clothes with; it was thick. And feeling the pressure return to my chest and legs, the cutter started to push the thorn through the raw flesh that remained of me, to sew together what was left. With each agonising stitch she sat back and admired her work before finally putting the thorn down and congratulating herself. 'Good, I've sealed it properly.'

I was exhausted, dizzy despite the fact I was lying down. Now the four women wrapped me from hip to toe in bandages, mummifying me from the waist down, and tying threads tightly at my hips, my knees and my ankles. I must have had the look of a blood-soaked mermaid. Slowly they lifted me just a few inches, flat on my back, from the crinkly mat on to a mattress beside it. As they did, my head fell to my left and my eyes caught sight of the cloth, dyed scarlet by my blood. There was something else beside it: a gooey, pinky pile of flesh. I closed my eyes; I couldn't look at what they'd taken from me.

My body leapt and bounced its protest, the shock finally sinking into every nerve and making its objection in jerky, uncontrollable movements.

'If you don't hold her down, the thread will come out and I will have to do it again,' I heard the far-off voice of the cutter say.

The fear would normally have kept me stock still, but my body was out of my control.

'Hold it Hibo, be brave,' my auntie said.

That word again – brave. The implication that I'd had some choice, that my mind might have been able to control itself, that I could have reacted differently to their butchering of me, that I might not have screamed as I was hacked at – if only I'd been brave enough.

All the women left the hut then, and I lay there alone, my body racked with pain. I heard them on the other side of the canvas, paying the cutter, saying goodbye. *Thanking* her.

Back inside the hut, I stared up at a tiny glint of sky that peeked through the thick canvas, a light blue now. My neighbours, my cousins would be waking up to a new day, going about their lives as normal. The children would be going to school, the men to work; the women would be busying themselves in the kitchen. But my life had changed forever. Something else had been severed along with the skin from my body, intangible but nevertheless real. This woman who claimed to be my mother was a fake and a fraud – she looked like my mother, she smelt like her, she sounded like her, but she wasn't my mother anymore. When she abandoned me in this hut, she abandoned me in this world. She was to become the object of my hate.

My brain was shattered, my screams all used up; even my eyes were too exhausted for tears to flow. They knew there was no point in trying to wash away the hurt and so instead they closed and I fell into sleep, desperate to escape this living nightmare.

5

The Aftermath

I don't know how long I slept, only that the sun was high in the sky when I woke and the hut offered me some shade from it out in the back of the yard, among the trees. The air was sticky with the scent of stale blood, and I heard flies buzzing above the canvas, the *loovan* that burned on the dish of charcoal keeping them away from me as I lay paralysed with pain. Instinctively, I pulled my arms up across my chest, linking my fingers and clasping them tightly over my breastbone, a sad little gesture; perhaps I was trying to protect myself, perhaps to comfort myself. The first thing that entered my fragmented mind was, of course, the pain. Everything from the waist down still burned like it was on fire, engulfing me, spreading out to my arms, my chest and finally banging at my temples.

The women must have been checking on me regularly, because I hadn't been awake for more than ten minutes before the canvas door opened and my aunt came in with a bottle of fizzy orange and a straw. She lifted my head just slightly from the mattress, and I winced even to be touched, even for my body to be moved a few millimetres.

'Just take two sips,' my auntie said.

I did as I was told and she left without saying another word. I was glad – I didn't want to talk to anyone. I didn't so much as try. My voice had been snatched by the horror of that morning, and even if I had wanted to speak, I'm not sure what I would have said. I didn't want to see anyone. Who would be there for me now anyway, when the women I trusted more than anyone else in the world had been party to such cruelty towards me? As I lay there under the canvas, the tears started. They kept on coming, I couldn't stop them, and I was in too much agony even to lift my hands to wipe them away. Who would wipe them away for me now? I had no one.

I heard voices outside the hut, the muted sounds of women cooking with one another, dogs barking, goats scuffing the ground a few feet away from me, the occasional bleat piercing an otherwise silent yard. My mind was in turmoil, replaying over and over the events of that morning, trying to make sense of it all. Why would Hoyo have done that? How could she have done that? Why had this happened to me? What had I done to deserve such a punishment?

She came into the hut after a couple of hours. I just lay there, staring up at the roof, refusing even to turn my face to her. She moved forward a few inches, leant over me and into my line of vision, but she wasn't the woman I had known for my whole life. She was a stranger.

'Hello, Hibo,' she spoke softly. 'How are you?'

My only answer to her was the tears that traced a long, slow line down my cheeks to my ears. Hoyo took her scarf and wiped them away, then stroked my face. I didn't want her to touch me. I wanted to recoil from her nearness, to retreat from her treacherous hands. Instead, all I could do was cry.

'You will be fine,' she said.

I turned my eyes to her then and I thought, *I won't be fine, not ever, not at all. Not after this.*

'I want to wee,' I croaked at last, and so she left the hut and returned with my auntie a few moments later. Very carefully, the two women lifted me off the ground and a few inches to the side while I still lay on my back. I cried out as white-hot bolts of pain coursed the length of my body. They placed me so that my bottom was over a hole they'd dug in the earth next to me that had been covered by leaves, my legs still tightly bound together in the cloth. 'Wee,' my auntie instructed me gently and I looked at her, my heart racing and my eyes conveying my confusion.

'How?' I said.

'Just let go of the wee and it will come,' she said.

So I did as she said, but it didn't come, nothing like it had before. And then when it did, it felt like I was on fire. What I didn't understand then was that I had been sewn from top to bottom. The skin

39

that was left after they'd sliced away my vaginal lips had been pulled tight over my urethra and sewn all the way down to my vagina itself, where a tiny hole – much smaller than the original – was all that was left. Where previously it had flowed quickly and freely, now my urine had to travel down to that hole, slowly trickling its descent like acid poured over the raw wound until drip . . . drip . . . drip . . . it finally started to leave my body. And I screamed, I screamed like I hadn't done for hours.

'It's OK, it's OK, it's OK,' my auntie reassured me repeatedly. But it was far from OK.

I was shaking again by the time they placed me back down on the mattress. I prayed to God that I would never have to wee again. *I am alive*, I thought, *but I wish I was dead*. I begged my mother and my aunt to give me something, anything to cool me down, to ease the pain. I begged them to pour cold water on my pelvis to take away the burning, even for a few seconds. But they refused.

When my aunt came back later with more fizzy orange, I knocked it out of her hand with a feeble swipe. The heat under the canvas must have been over 30 degrees, but I was too terrified of passing urine again to take another sip of drink.

'Are you hot, Hibo?' she asked.

I nodded. Yet I refused to drink, so instead she brought ice cubes and rubbed them over my forehead, across my lips.

On my own again, with the fading daylight came some respite at last from the heat. I took my mind off the stabbing, shrieking, incessant pains by watching soft white smoke from the burning *loovan* snake into the air above me, swirling and curling in patterns, making a silvery trail up to the tiny hole in the roof of the canvas where the sticks met. The woody scent, a little like pine, was some comfort, and if I closed my eyes I could pretend I was lying in a forest, a long way from this mattress, and these binds that cut into my knees and ankles.

I tried to focus not on the pain, but on getting better. As soon as I was better, I would find out why this had happened to me. In those hot nights I was to spend alone over the following weeks, a thin piece of cloth covering my body, I vowed that I would ask my mother every day until she told me the truth.

Two days later, I was allowed to eat something for the first time. Just two or three sips of soup, my auntie holding the spoon up to my lips and helping me to sit up a little so that I could drink it down. I'd existed on the shock of the trauma alone – the last thing I'd thought of was eating, the pain still a heavy knot in my stomach, replacing any appetite I might have had even if they'd tried to feed me. Which, of course, they didn't because I was bound from hip to toe: it was impossible to go to the toilet even if I'd wanted to, and they encouraged me to do the bare minimum.

My mother had wandered in and out of the hut as I drifted in and out of sleep. Each time she spoke to me, I stared straight ahead, up at the gap in the canvas. My body was in that hut, my mind far away. If she offered me a drink, no matter how thirsty I was, I wouldn't accept anything from her. She was a fraud and a traitor.

The smell from the hole in the ground beside me where the women lifted me over to wee was awful. They covered it over with leaves, but nothing could disguise the stench of the urine in that searing heat. The *loovan* masked it slightly, but it couldn't take it away.

After a few more days, my cousins came into the hut to say hello to me. I didn't want to speak to them. They went away.

Then, on the fifth day, my auntie brought in some rice and milk on a spoon.

'Please, Hibo,' she said. 'Please eat a little something.' I refused. She went away and came back a few moments later; this time it was covered with honey to tempt me. I took one spoonful but I couldn't so much as chew it; my body was rejecting even a mouthful of food, and as the days went by I grew weaker and weaker. But my mind, my mind was strong.

And then, on the tenth day, the cutter returned. When I looked up and saw her enter the hut – those eyes, those pincer nails – I decided that today would be a good day to die. If I could have run, I would have, but my legs were still tightly bound by the cloth. She placed her stall in front of me again as my mother hovered behind her, and my tiny heart pounded in terror inside my chest, as she slowly started to unpeel the dressing.

'Open your legs,' she said, after she'd removed the bandages. 'I won't hurt you.'

As if I was going to trust this woman, the same one I'd cursed time and again in my head since that morning ten days ago. I'd decided she must be a *sheydan* – a devil. How could she cause so much pain to a child with such a complete absence of remorse?

The Aftermath

After the binding had been unpeeled, try as I might to protect myself, to keep my legs clenched shut, she forced them apart with little real effort. I caught sight of the dull glint of the razors again and I begged God then please just to take me. Let me die now. I screamed and screamed, deaf to the cutter's words. 'I'm not going to touch you. I just need to take these stitches out.'

The pain as she cut at each knot with the razor, dragging the thread through skin that was still raw, was unbearable. In my head, I cursed her a thousand more times. I called her all the names that my six-year-old brain could conjure up. *You devil woman*, I thought deep inside, my body weak but my eyes trying to burn my insults into her skin. *You deserve to die for what you did to me! You're nasty! You're evil!*

When it was over, she gathered together her wicked tools again and raised herself up from her little seat. Before she left, she gave me a final hard stare with those terrifying eyes. She had a message for me: 'You don't speak of this. You never tell other girls about it.'

I was shaking then. It was difficult to know whether it was through fear or anger.

And then my mother said: 'If you talk about it you will look like someone who is not brave enough, people will see you as a coward, and you've been very brave.'

I didn't want to speak about it ever again, not what they'd done or how they'd done it. I never wanted to think about the pain ever, or those days spent in that hut alone.

I only wanted to know why.

*

That day, after those crude stitches had been removed at last, I tried to stand for the first time since the cutting. But ten days with little food and drink had left me weak and wasted. Just one look at my arms told me how much weight had dropped off me as I'd lain in that hut, under the scorching Somalian sun. I had always been a slight and skinny child, but now the bones in my hands jutted visibly against my skin, and my wrists had been whittled down to twigs. It needed both my mother and my auntie to grip an arm each and walk me out of the hut and around the yard. I blinked hard as the full force of the sun's rays hit me for the first time in almost two weeks.

Later my auntie held me over a tin bath while my mother sponged water over me. She was gentle, but her touch felt a world away from that last bath she'd given me, a mockery of the role she had once played. My skin bristled at the feel of her hands on my body. I wanted it over with; I wanted to go back to the safety of my hut, the small space that had been my security while I'd recovered. It hurt to walk; even if my muscles remembered what to do, my joints still stung from where my auntie and the cutter's assistant had pulled at my legs, and in between my legs . . . in between my legs . . . I couldn't bring myself to think about what they'd done there.

My mother brought out one of the new dresses from my party for me and slipped it on over my head as I sat there, scrawny arms aloft. None of the clothes looked as lovely in this new light as they had when I first received them. Now, they represented a betrayal. Those presents, the congratulations, it had all been a trick. I couldn't imagine a day when I would ever eat *halwa* again.

My mother and my auntie tried to feed me up again, but I didn't want to eat. I didn't want to speak. I decided then I would never call my mother by her name again. I was up on my feet, but the world looked completely different now.

6

The Truth at Last

*E*ach and every morning that followed after my *gudnin*, I
would look my mother square in the eyes and ask, 'Why?
Why did this happen to me?' On good days she would tell me to go
and play in the yard; on bad days, I would see a flash of irritation
in her eyes and she would chase me around the house to get rid of
me, picking up any object she could find along the way to shoo me
out. Some days she would simply ignore me, and it was then that
I'd feel most angry. I'd wonder how she could dismiss what had
happened to me so easily, but she did. Whichever way my mother
responded, she never gave me the answer I sought, and I would
vow again to ask the following day, and the one after that, and the
one after that.

I never asked her to do anything for me, I never said hello or goodbye or goodnight. I never even called her Hoyo. The woman who cooked my meals, who saved an extra can of fizzy orange for me in the fridge, who never told me off if I walked home from school slower than the others, she was not my mother. She was a shadow of the woman whom I once called Hoyo – a shadow of the woman who had always answered my incessant questions about the world outside of our compound and who'd always laughed at my curiosity. Now I had only one question, and I could see from her face that she dreaded my asking it.

I could still think back to a time when she had indulged me and my inquisitive nature. I could still remember the day when she told me that there were people in the world who had pale skin, much paler than ours. She told me they were called 'white people'.

'What do they call us?' I'd asked, my eyes wide.

'Black,' she'd said.

And then I argued: 'I'm not black, why do they call me black? My skin is brown. I'm not black!' And she'd thrown her head back and laughed.

I remembered going with her to visit a relative in hospital, and how as we walked the corridors one of these white people appeared ahead of us. I saw her legs and gasped and pulled at my mother's hand in mine. 'She's not white, Hoyo, she's pink! Why do people say she is white? White is this wall. She is not white.' And Hoyo had laughed again. I remember the pink woman had given me a lollipop, and I'd decided these pink people were nice after all, even if they couldn't get their colours right.

But that was another life. There was no laughter between us

anymore, there was no talk. She still tucked me up in bed at night, even when I was almost eight, but when she bent down to kiss my forehead just like she had always done, I moved my face away or covered myself over with the sheet.

I'd answer to my aunties, I'd smile and talk and even give them hugs, and I'd look over their shoulder as I did and see the hurt in my mother's eyes. And they'd say: 'You can hug your mother too, you know?'

And I'd reply: 'I know, but I don't want to.'

'Why?' they'd ask. I wouldn't answer; they knew why. As far as I was concerned, my mother had forfeited the right to be close to me when she chose to look the other way instead of answer my pleas. I hated her, deep inside, and no passage of time, no wounded expressions or entreaties from my aunties would change that. Nothing could shake my sense that all the affection, all the love, all the patience she had shown me had been a deception.

Each day took me further away from the horror of that hut, and yet the memory of it was still branded on my mind. It wasn't just to my mother that I looked for answers in those weeks and months that followed; it was to the other girls in the school playground, the ones with whom I walked to and from *madrasa*. Sometimes I'd find a group of my friends sitting on the yellow ground, the earth's dust streaking their long skirts, and I'd say to them: 'Why did they do it? Why did they cut us?' And one by one they'd stand up and walk away, or they'd stare at the ground as if it offered an escape from my questions. I guessed that they'd been given the same warning as me: never discuss this with anyone. And yet when I think about it, who really does talk about such intimate things in the open air of the playground? Why did I think anyone would ever tell me why it had happened?

I lost count of the number of nights I woke up screaming from nightmares, my face covered in a film of sweat, and my cousins standing at the foot of my bed, telling me that it was OK, it was only a dream. I'd wipe my own face and go back to sleep, but whenever I closed my eyes I'd see the images of that day playing out on the inside of my eyelids.

Repeated urine infections were brought on by the fact that my urethra was sealed over, which meant I was constantly being taken to hospital to be treated with antibiotics, as were all the other girls I knew. And still we never spoke to one another about what had happened. They didn't seem as keen as me to understand what had been done to us; they didn't seem to feel as alone or as burdened by this great, heavy secret. So I learned not to talk to anyone. I never went to another *gudnin* party, though – I couldn't be part of the lie; I wouldn't pretend it was just a little cut.

The years gathered pace and my relationship with my mother continued to deteriorate. It was almost ten years after the cutting when I awoke one night and felt wet between my legs. I'd got up in the darkness, tiptoeing my way to the bathroom, but I hadn't wet myself in my sleep. I climbed back into bed and drifted off again. But the following morning when I pulled down my knickers to go to the toilet, the gusset was dyed scarlet, and terror tore through me. I was bleeding, down there. I had to be dying.

I rushed back to my room and checked my sheets – they, too, were covered in blood. By the time my cousin Fatima found me, I was hysterical.

'What's wrong?' she said, surely seeing the stricken expression on my face.

'I'm dying,' I told her. 'I'm dying!'

She tried to calm me, to stop me from pacing the room, but the panic had claimed every rational thought I had.

'Shut up and sit down,' Fatima said, in an attempt to get some sense out of me. 'Now, why do you think you're dying?'

I took a deep breath. 'There's blood . . . in my knickers,' I told her. 'I don't know what's happening to me. I don't want to die!'

Her expression lightened as realisation dawned, and she sat down on the bed next to me. 'You're not dying, Hibo,' she said. 'You're becoming a woman.'

'What do you mean "becoming a woman"? I'm not a boy! I'm nearly sixteen, I *am* a woman.'

'No, Hibo, you were a *girl* – until now,' she said.

My face must have shown my confusion, because she sighed in exasperation and then tried again. 'When you get your period it means you become a woman, and you can get pregnant.' She crossed the room and pulled out a piece of cloth from a drawer.

'This is mine,' she said. 'Use this inside your knickers and keep washing it out. If you don't, the blood will seep through your clothes and everyone will see.'

I took the cloth from her and stared at it. It was clearly from an old dress of hers – I faintly recognised the faded striped pattern that ran through it.

'Does Hoyo bleed?' I asked her.

'Yes, all women do. Now go and wash your bedding.'

I stripped my bed and took the sheets out into the yard, washing them in a tub of cool soapy water. My mother found me out there, and when she saw the blood she started whooping with happiness, making the sound usually reserved for weddings, a call women make in celebration.

'Why are you making that noise?' I asked. 'It's not a wedding.'

'Because you're a woman now.'

I know she told my aunties because from across the yard I saw them pointing and congratulating my mother, patting her back and throwing their arms around her with joy. I watched them, confused, the cloth firmly held in my knickers, and wincing with each stomach cramp that came in waves across my belly. What did this mean 'to be a woman'? And why did it always seem to involve pain?

'Why are they so happy?' I asked Fatima.

'Because you got your period,' she sighed, and turned back to sweeping the yard. 'You really need to stop your brain asking questions, Hibo.'

So this was the next stage – there was clearly a distinction between being a girl and being a woman – and unknowingly and involuntarily I had transitioned through the first two phases. I had been cut and now I bled. So what was next? And what would it cost?

*

I got used to the pain that would grip my insides every twenty-eight days. I also came to understand that without a proper hole for the menstrual blood to exit my body, the flood would build up inside me, and I would be doubled over at times, in agony for ten days, sometimes for two long weeks. I learned to dread my periods just as I had learned to wait patiently for the slow trickle when I urinated.

And still I didn't know why I needed to suffer as I did, still my mother refused to answer my daily question. Until one day, a few months after my sixteenth birthday, on a day that seemed like any other, I got a response that differed from my mother's usual dismissal. I'd had a shower that day and had styled my hair differently in two tight ponytails. As I came out of the bathroom, steam rising off my skin, my mother looked up from her sewing.

'You look pretty, Hibo,' she said. 'I like the way you've done your hair today.'

I don't know what it was, perhaps my new hairstyle had softened me around the edges a little, but I felt myself smiling a reply to her. And in response, her face relaxed, the tension eased for a moment. It was a tiny gesture on both our parts, a truce of sorts in a ten-year struggle. I decided then that this was my chance.

'Why did you do this to me?' I asked, as I had on every single day before that. I wasn't expecting an answer; I was expecting her to fix that same hard look on her face and say nothing. Instead, she gestured for me to sit down opposite her. I did as she indicated, encouraged by this new and different response from her. I waited for her to speak.

'You're sixteen now, so I will tell you,' she said.

She spoke slowly, as if she too realised the importance of what she was about to share. 'I was cut, your grandmother was cut, and every mother before her. And your children will be cut too.'

I listened intently, ready to absorb her every word.

'We are a family whose girls are known for our virginity. We are clean, and that means we can marry well, and you will stay pure until you get married to your husband.'

I struggled to digest what she'd said, and so I tried to undo all the words before reordering them into some kind of sense, some kind of an explanation. I waited for her to say more, but instead she turned back to her sewing. That was it?

'But why was it done?' I demanded.

She looked down at her work.

'And why was it so painful? What did that woman take from me?'

'I've told you now,' she said, without looking up. 'Never ask me again.'

And with that the conversation was over before it had even begun. That was it – that short exchange of words was all that I had to sate me after all these years. But it served only to make me hungrier for answers, to leave me with more whys, and each one led to another, and another, and another. I wanted to know why I had been mutilated.

I remember that day so vividly. How I went over and over everything that my mother had told me. How in class, sitting behind my school desk, I'd chewed my pen almost frantically, trying to work out what it all meant. At breaktime, I didn't stand and chat with my friends; all I could think about was trying to fill in the missing gaps. I'd gone through so much pain because the women in my family had done so before me – that wasn't an explanation. I had gone through all this suffering for marriage, to stay pure for a man. What did she mean *'for* a man'? I looked around at the boys in my class, and wondered why I needed to be pure for them, and why what they thought of me mattered so much. Girls had to be 'preserved', subjected to all this pain and disfigurement – to the extent that even basic bodily functions like urinating and menstruating became difficult – all for a man.

But I didn't care what he would think of me, some nameless, faceless man I'd never laid eyes on. I only cared about the body that had been chopped and cut and mutilated. My body. I'd heard enough tales about girls who had gone into those huts and never come out. I thought about all those girls who, like me, were showered with gifts and food and parties, but whose own *gudnin* hadn't gone to plan. 'It was God's way,' is how the women put it, discarding their lives with just a few words. And all that, the blood, the flesh, the loss of life, that was all for a man?

I thought then of my cousins, and the other girls I'd known who had got married, and I remembered how after their wedding we'd hear whispers that they weren't sleeping in their marital bed, but in a hospital one instead. It happened to every single girl without fail. And months later, when they finally returned to visit, they were gaunt and skeletal, all light gone from their eyes. What had happened to them?

CUT

My cousin Fatima was two years older than me, so we always knew she would get married before me. Fatima was excited, but as our other cousins talked about the engagement party I saw fear in her too. Of course she wanted to marry – she wanted to have her own home, and a family of her own – but she knew, too, that her wedding would probably be followed by a hospital visit, even if we didn't understand why.

When her wedding celebrations came around she was taken to visit various relatives, who gave her beautiful-smelling treatments to smooth her hair and lighten her face, and drew delicate henna designs on her fingers. The day before the ceremony we sat cross-legged in our bedroom for what would be our last night together. As the day had come closer I'd become more worried for her.

'Please come back and tell me what happens after the wedding,' I begged her, taking her hands in mine. 'No one else will tell me.'

We were both crying.

'I don't want you to go to hospital,' I said, kissing her.

'I'm scared, Hibo,' she said. 'I don't want to go to hospital either.'

'Promise me you'll tell me,' I pleaded.

She nodded.

'You have to promise on the Koran.'

I crossed the room and picked up a copy. With shaking hands, she did as I asked.

The wedding day was a huge celebration and I watched along with the rest of my family as the traditional red-and-black head-dress – the *shash* – was placed on her head by the older women, a sign that she was now married. But I didn't whoop in celebration for Fatima, because I was too terrified for her. Nobody is allowed to visit the bride and groom for the first seven days after they are married, but it didn't stop me asking my family if they had any news of my cousin. I just wanted to know if she was OK, but nobody would tell me anything. Nor did I hear anything on the grapevine; this time there were not even any whispers, at least not any that reached me.

I'd lie in bed at night and look over at her empty bed. 'Where are you?' I'd ask the darkness.

Each day, for weeks, I'd ask my aunties when Fatima would come to see us.

'She'll come when she's ready,' was a stock reply.

'She's busy with her husband,' was another.

I knew in the pit of my stomach that she was sick, of course I knew, the ties that bound us so tightly were stronger than the miles anyone could put between us, but I was helpless; all I could do was pray that she would come soon. Fatima's name had just disappeared from everyone's lips, and when they did speak of her it was in hushed mutterings.

And then finally, after three long months she came home to our villa. But the tall and beautiful girl I'd said goodbye to had gone, and in her place was a woman who had lost so much weight her cheekbones jutted out at sharp angles from her skull, her eyes sinking into the void that they left. Fatima had always been happy, carefree, forever helping her mother out in the house, nodding in concentration as her mother taught her how to apply kohl to her eyes in the months before she was ready to be married. Now she was like a ghost flitting between the rooms of our villa where once she'd darted in and out, laughing. I looked at her and all I could see was misery.

I held on to her hand and pulled her to follow me into our old bedroom. Once we were there I shut the door and we sat down on my bed, just like we always had – except now, everything had changed. The sun shone in through the window shutter in slices, casting fragmented shadows on her drawn features, her hollowed cheeks. I threw my arms around her, feeling her ribs sticking out under my hug, both of us swallowing hot tears.

'What happened?' I asked her. 'Why do you look like this?'

She looked down.

'Remember you promised,' I said.

'I was sick, I was in hospital,' she said.

'But why? You have a beautiful new house and a good husband, don't you?'

'Yes, Hibo,' she said. 'I have a nice husband but you have no idea what awaits you.'

I sat back, frightened of what I was about to hear.

'You know how we go to the toilet and we can't even wee?'

I nodded, slowly.

'Imagine you have a rolling pin, and then imagine that going through you . . . down there.'

I looked at her, confused. 'Why would a rolling pin go in there?'

She swallowed hard.

'I'm comparing something to a rolling pin,' she said. 'You know your husband, he is the rolling pin . . . I don't know how to tell you

58

this, Hibo, but you have to sleep with your husband ... He has a thing, and that thing becomes bigger, like a rolling pin, and that has to go through your tiny hole. That's what they call sex.'

What did I know about sex or the acts that men and women commit in the name of love? My mother had certainly never told me. Fatima knew this, of course, because she would have been just as naive on her wedding night as I was now. The women would have taken her aside at some point after the ceremony, once she was wed; they would have told her gently, but with little fuss, that she had duties to perform for her husband – that was the deal, the bargain for a ring on her finger and a home away from us. That was the price she would need to pay. And still she would not have understood, not until she was on that bed, with him approaching her. We were pure – as my mother had said, women in our family were known for their purity. She saw me floundering in possession of this new information and tried to explain it another way.

I stared at her, still uncomprehending.

'... I tore badly and I caught an infection, that's why I was in hospital.'

Everything around me just crashed, that's the only way I can describe it.

'They cut us to make sure the men find us like that.'

And then, horrifyingly, the final piece of the jigsaw puzzle fell into place. My mother had told me that she wanted to preserve my virginity, that our family were known for being clean, and I hadn't understood properly what virginity was, until now.

I let go of Fatima's hand then, and I staggered to the other side of the room. I sat on the floor in the corner and put my head between my knees. I rocked there, back and forth, praying a million times over that the same thing wouldn't happen to me. *I'd rather die than go through that*, I thought. And in that split second I hated men.

'The pain hasn't finished,' Fatima was saying. 'There is more to come.'

Why was it my fate to be born a woman? I was in a nightmare and there was no escape. By now I was only catching the odd few words, as my thoughts ricocheted off the walls of my mind – 'Lying on the bed in a pool of blood ... Making noises like a wounded animal ... His family dancing around the bed ... Congratulating him on how pure you are ...'

I looked up at her, my face aghast as the horror of it washed over me in waves. This is what was waiting for me, to be torn open all over again, by someone else? I had survived the cutting, only to be served a second punishment? The fear had taken hold of my brain and with its grasping spindly fingers it was squeezing, squeezing, squeezing. Please God, I begged. I don't want to be in pain any-more. I pleaded, I bargained, I begged. I prayed.

'Hibo ...' I felt my cousin put her arm around my shoulders, as she sat down gingerly beside me again. 'You said you wanted to know.'

And I did, I did want to know. We were kept pure for men, and then broken in by them. And what happened to us in the meantime was completely irrelevant in the pursuit of their pleasure, or their integrity, their masculinity. Were females really valued so little? Would my own daughters face the same fate?

I was back in that hut, on that raging river of pain and unable to get off because this was my life, this was my destiny. I would be married to one of my scruffy cousins – I will have been deformed, defiled, kept pure for him, so he can open me up again, and then my daughter will be chopped and maimed for her own husband and, just like my mother told me, there would be nothing I could do about it because it has happened to every woman before us. I sobbed and sobbed – for myself, for my daughters, for all the women and girls in Somalia, past, present and future.

If only I could have vowed then that I would change the future, that I wouldn't let what befell Fatima happen to me, but I knew it was out of my hands; it was what I was born into. And so I decided in that moment that I would rather die than face the same fate, endure more pain, and that I would protect any daughters of mine from the same.

And this was a promise I intended to keep.

7

Freedom

From up in the clouds, the lights below twinkled a starry welcome to me. My forehead had been stuck to the tiny window of the aeroplane since we'd taken off from Nairobi. As the plane had lifted up from the ground, I'd waved goodbye to the arid land beneath me, and watched the eight-hour movie that whizzed by at my window. We'd soared up above the clouds into the deep blue sky, each hour bringing me closer to Britain, to freedom. I hadn't slept for the flight like most of my fellow passengers; instead, I'd kept upright in my seat, not wanting to miss a minute of the journey that would change my life.

I was eighteen when that plane took off from Kenya. Never in my wildest dreams had I imagined ever leaving Somalia, but then civil war had broken out in our country and our president was overthrown. None of the tribes could agree on a replacement for him, and fighting between rival factions meant that the country could not deal with natural disasters like drought and therefore famine. The stories of homes that were broken into during the night, girls who were raped in front of their parents by militia, had grown increasingly loud and increasingly close in the months that preceded my father sending my mother, my brother and sister and me to Kenya. He thought it would be just until the country settled down, and we'd gone into Kenya illegally and without paperwork. Our villa had been the only home I'd known, life in Mogadishu was all that I'd ever known, but the day I was told we were leaving the country that had brutalised me was one of the best of my life. Who would have thought that out of such destruction could come the freedom I'd longed for?

In Kenya we had been refugees, travelling from home to home without paperwork, at risk every day we spent in Nairobi of being sent back to possible death, and yet I was never scared, not as scared as I would have been back in my homeland. That country might have been my home, but, as far as I was concerned, it had betrayed me and every other woman like me.

To be a feminist as an African woman in those days was an unusual thing, but when I look back now there is no other word to describe the person I was. As a child I'd questioned why my mother was happy to cook and clean for the family, why she had no ambitions of her own. And she would tell me: 'Those are not jobs for women. Your place is with your husband, with your children.' I never understood that as a child, and as a teenager I was appalled by the idea, because I'd known from just a few years old that I didn't want to be my mother. I wanted to be something more than her. It wasn't just because of what she'd done to me; it was the way she viewed womanhood, as if it were only something truly satisfying as long as there was a man to take you and accept you, someone for you to cook and clean for. It started off as a feeling for me, that desire to be something more than my mother, and over the years as my hatred for her grew it became a determined act of defiance. I would be more than a wife and a mother. I felt as though each mile that took me further from Somalia would give me the opportunity to be more than her.

I loved Nairobi. The roads were tarmacked, so different from the dusty, unfinished ones back in Mogadishu, and the houses had an upstairs. I loved the tall buildings, and the green parks where people took rowing boats out on the lake.

Even though Hadsan was married, my mother had insisted we weren't leaving Somalia without her. So there was me, Hoyo, Hadsan, two of my cousins and my brother. Hadsan's husband followed us out there, and we relied on the generosity of friends and family to keep us hidden from the authorities. Each time the police found us, we managed to send them away with the money they wanted, but whatever they asked for only bought us twenty-four hours before they'd be knocking again at whatever new door we were then hiding behind. It wasn't an easy life, but, as far as I was concerned, it was still better than Somalia.

After we'd been staying with friends in Nairobi for a year, my father phoned my mother in the middle of the night. In the morning, when she sat us down, fatigue had carved deep grooves beneath her eyes, and she looked older than I'd remembered from the night before.

'Your father says you are to make your own lives now,' my mother told us. 'He said we can't go back to Mogadishu.'

If I'd shared a closer bond with my mother, if it hadn't been broken, I might have wanted to stay with her, but when I knew I was free to go wherever I wanted to claim asylum as a refugee, I couldn't wait to leave her side. Ninety per cent of Somalians were choosing Canada, my people were leaving on planes in their thousands. But I didn't want to go there – there was a name that appealed to me more than anywhere, a word that sounded so different, so intriguing, so interesting: London.

'I want to go to London,' I told my mother.

So when my mother heard of a family friend, Zahara, who was flying to London, she agreed I could go with her. Zahara was in her thirties, an older, responsible person for my eighteen-year-old self to travel with, to be my chaperone as I headed up into the sky on a new adventure. But to me, leaving Africa didn't just mean safety from the civil war; it meant freedom from my own culture. It meant saving my life.

The plane circled the airport before making its descent, and then finally I heard the captain address us over the Tannoy: 'Ladies and gentlemen, welcome to London Heathrow.' I had arrived. Hibo had arrived, and I knew this was just the beginning. Tears started running down my face.

I was *free*.

I was free.

'Don't you want to be here?' asked Zahara, seeing my tears.

But I wanted it more than anything I'd ever wanted before.

We disembarked, but not to the balmy evening we'd left in Nairobi. Instead, there was a breeze so cold that when I arrived at the plane doors to exit, the shock of it pushed me back into the aircraft. Goosebumps stood to attention on my arms like they never had before.

'Are you OK?' the stewardess said.

I looked down at the long trousers I had on and the thin shirt, and she immediately seemed to understand I was too terrified of the cold to step outside. She kept me on board until all the other passengers had filtered off, and then Zahara gave me her denim jacket and one of her big scarves. But even as I walked carefully down the stairs, seeing the lights of the night shimmering against the tarmac, my teeth were chattering. Inside the airport terminal, out of the cruelty of the wind, I asked Zahara if I could stop to use the first toilet we saw, and in there I burst into tears again. A million thoughts raced through my mind: this is freedom, this is my life now. I will choose who I love; I will choose who I marry. But, most importantly, I would choose not to have my own daughters cut. Just by arriving in this country, I had saved future babies from mutilation and I cried because there was no other feeling of freedom like it. I knew from that moment on I would decide everything and be in charge of my life in this new land, with these pink people who call themselves white. And even then, I knew one of the first things I was going to ask for: to be opened.

When I came out of the toilet, Zahara was waiting for me.

'Why are you crying again?' she asked.

'I'm just so happy,' I told her.

We followed the last of the crowds from the plane towards a large area where a huge queue of people snaked its way round the room. There, two police officers came towards us, and we handed them the fake passports with which we'd travelled and embarked the plane. We told them the word we'd been taught to say back in Kenya, the only English word we knew then: 'Asylum.' And they indicated for us to follow them. They took us to a room and motioned for us to sit. It was difficult to know whether I was shaking with nerves or from the cold, but one of the police officers saw I was shivering and handed me his jacket, then he came back with two steaming coffees for us. They were so kind, right from the start, and although I realised that my life was in their hands until we made it out of the airport, I never worried they'd send us back to Kenya.

Eventually a woman called Margaret appeared – she was an older woman, maybe fifty, and her face was lined with kindness. She spoke a few words of Somali, enough to ask our names and how old we were. She asked if we were hungry and I nodded so hard I felt sure my head might roll straight off my shoulders. She left the room and returned with a tuna sandwich and a banana, which I ate quickly. A few moments later she reappeared, this time with a man who would be our translator. The immigration officers sat in front of us, with Biros and serious set faces, and wrote down on a form everything our translator reported back to them. They wanted to know everything about us: where we were from, why we left, where our parents were, if we had any siblings.

The questions were exhausting and endless, and when eventually they'd finished the translator explained to us that Margaret would be taking us to a hostel in London. There we would receive income support – £25 a week – while they processed our application for asylum. Finally, after a whole day spent in the airport, we were on our way, and I sat in the back of Margaret's small car, watching the lights of London loom bigger and brighter towards us. I was here in this city which sounded so wonderful, and to me everything about it was beautiful and so different from anything I'd ever seen. It was December when we arrived in the UK and as we got out of the car, snow crunched under my feet. I looked down at it, mesmerised by the whiteness of it, and when I bent down and picked it up between two fingers, the delight on my face must have been obvious because Margaret laughed before beckoning me to follow her into the hostel.

Cecil House was right in the centre of London, in an area called Holborn; it was a dark-brown brick tenement building with white sash windows. Anyone else might have thought it was an ugly-looking place, but to me it represented the first bed that I'd slept in without my mother on the other side of my door, and for no other reason than that I thought it was wonderful. But I was tired, so tired, and when Margaret showed me the room I'd be sleeping in with another Somalian girl, which had two single beds and our own toilet, I crawled straight on to one of the beds. I cuddled myself up within the duvet, the first I'd ever seen in my life, and, wrapped up in this warm cloud, I stopped shivering for the first time as sleep took me far away in my dreams, to the only place they knew, the dusty streets of Mogadishu that had once been so familiar.

Margaret returned the next day and took me shopping, and I fell in love with London that day as we walked down Oxford Street, Margaret pointing out all the Christmas decorations that twinkled and shimmered above my head. I'd never seen anything so beautiful before. In London, as if to embrace this new sense of freedom, for a time I abandoned the headscarf I'd worn since I was a little girl.

In the days that followed, I got to know more of the other Somalian girls at the hostel. It was strange how tribal everyone was: despite the fact that we were miles from our homeland, the girls from northern Somalia only wanted to speak to other northern girls, which left me with the girls who, like me, were from the south. Except they weren't like me at all, they weren't young and naive – Nasra and Habiba were ten years older and a lot more confident. They'd been living in Italy for six or more years so they were used to the Western way of things. Unlike me, they didn't marvel at the fact there were flushing toilets in the hostel, standing and flushing them over and over, wondering where the water might go, or stare astonished as a seemingly endless supply of water shot from taps after just one little turn. They also looked cool. Nasra had a white Afro and Habiba had bright-red hair, and I felt so juvenile with my long black hair, which Hoyo had allowed to grow down to my bottom. Inspired by Nasra and Habiba, I took a pair of scissors to it, chopping it away until it reached my neck. I put the pile of hair at my feet into the bin, and along with it some memories of my mother.

'What have you done?' Nasra asked me the following day. 'We loved your hair!'

But I didn't care; it would grow back and, anyway, I loved my new short bob.

We'd go out walking in the late afternoon, exploring the streets of London. Every time I'd see a dress covered in sequins in a shop window, I'd long for it, stopping to admire it.

'I wish it was mine,' I'd say.

And the girls would tease me. 'You're addicted to sparkly things,' they'd sigh.

There was a whole range of different women at the hostel, not just African girls like us, but English ones too. There was one older woman, who never told me her name, but she must have been in her seventies. She was beautifully dressed and wore colourful beaded necklaces that rattled on her chest every time she moved. She made jewellery and I used some of my income support to buy her beads. I wanted to try everything this country had to offer – short hair, jeans, beads, the lot. Many days I'd waste just trying on clothes in shops, twirling in the changing-room mirror in tops that showed my midriff. I felt like anything was possible, and it was. First, though, I had to free myself physically.

I'd been in the hostel for two weeks when I asked to see a doctor. The lady who ran the hostel booked an appointment for me at a GP's surgery around the corner, and I went along on my own, determined not to tell the other women what I wanted; instinct told me not to share my secret. We had never discussed *gudnin* in Somalia, and I knew it would be no different in London.

I walked into the surgery, and up to the receptionist's desk. As I waited in the queue I looked around the room, at the white walls covered with colourful posters, containing words that meant nothing to me. On hard chairs sat patients waiting with serious faces, some flicking through old magazines, mothers chastising their children for not keeping still, all of them so aware of the process, so familiar with their surroundings, the sterile smell, the hush that hung heavy in the room. When my name was called, I took a deep breath and went through the door the receptionist gestured towards. The doctor was sitting behind her desk wearing a warm smile, red jacket and black trousers. Her lips were pink and her eyes were blue, and she had painted blue mascara on to her lashes, which mesmerised me, momentarily distracting me from my purpose.

'How can I help?' she said.

'No English,' I told her, swiping my hands outwards.

So in turn she touched her head, her arms, her stomach. 'Does it hurt here? Here? Here?' she asked.

I shook my head, then tentatively pointed down between my legs. She nodded, understanding. She stood up from behind her desk and led me over to a couch, motioning for me to take off my trousers and get up on to the bed.

I did as she said, noticing, as I unzipped my jeans, that my hands were shaking; my heart was pounding against my chest so loudly that I was sure she would hear it. I climbed on to the couch and lay down, staring at the stucco tiles on the ceiling, trying to mentally bat away the images that flooded into my mind, because suddenly and quite unexpectedly I was six years old again, on my back, naked from the waist down, exposed. One after the other the images came: the sight of my mother beside me, my auntie pulling at my leg, the cutter's strange eyes, my fear. My hands shook violently. My knees stayed clamped together as I tried to breathe, slowly in, slowly out. I had wanted so much to be here, to get help, and now I wondered how that might happen when I couldn't bring myself to open my legs and allow the doctor to examine me.

The doctor saw my distress.

'It's OK,' she said gently, touching my knee. 'Can you open?' and she gestured with her hands, as if miming opening a book.

I tried, really I did, but the images were coming harder and faster.

'It's OK, it's OK,' she said again.

But all I could see was the cutter, slowly adjusting her scarf, dipping her hands in the kettle of water, those two long pincer nails . . .

I took another deep breath, and then another. *You're here now, Hibo*, I told myself. Let her help you – this is your chance. So somehow, ever so slowly, I allowed my legs to fall apart, just a few millimetres at first, her hands gently guiding them. And then finally, I was exposed and she saw for herself what I'd never yet dared to see with my own eyes. Skin snipped away, a hole just the size of a matchstick where my vagina should be. All other evidence of my femininity deleted and stitched over.

I burst into tears, just at the thought of what she saw before her, and feeling so ashamed of the way I looked, of the way they'd left me. I didn't want this doctor to think I was a freak, because that's how I thought of myself. She handed me a tissue, and then she went over to the small sink in her room, splashed water on to her face and dried it with a paper towel, before turning back to me. Noticing that she was so moved by what she'd seen somehow made me feel like I had an ally, that at last someone could see what they'd done to me back in Somalia. For the first time since I was six years old, someone was sympathising with me. Just her look told me that, and suddenly I wasn't frightened anymore.

She nodded and gestured to me to get dressed, and handed me an appointment card for 3:30pm the following day.

'Are you OK?' she asked, taking my arm before I left her office. And I nodded. 'OK,' I repeated, because I trusted her.

I didn't go straight back to the hostel after I left the surgery – I needed to gather myself together before I went home, because I knew that if anyone there found out what I was planning there would be repercussions. As I sat in a nearby park, watching the male pigeons dance around the females in an attempt to woo them, I understood that something now separated me from those other girls at the hostel. In sharing this secret with that doctor and showing her what had been done to me, I had taken the first step towards speaking out. For the second time in my life, I knew it was about to change irrevocably.

I couldn't sleep that night. I lay there in my bed, watching the beams of vehicle lights flicker across the walls of my room and listening to the sounds of the street. Perhaps it was the excitement that was keeping me awake, and perhaps it was the fear of what might happen the next day, when I returned to the surgery. It was probably a combination of both.

The following afternoon, back in the GP's waiting room, I sat across from another more official-looking Somalian woman. I guessed she was my translator. We smiled and said hello, but nothing more, although I could tell from the way her eyes crinkled when she smiled that she was a kind woman. She must have been in her thirties, and was dressed in a very Western way, smart with long trousers, and she had a wide smile underneath a red *hijab*.

A few moments later we were both called into the doctor's office and I felt relief, not fear, to see this kind doctor again. She spoke and in turn the translator said to me in Somali: 'The doctor wants to know what you want her to do.'

So I told her: 'I want her to open me.' And I watched, seemingly in slow motion, as my words took away the smile and replaced it with a look as if I'd just slapped her across the face.

'What do you mean "open"?' she asked.

'I want the doctor to open me up down there,' I said. 'Can you tell her?'

'No! What do you want to do that for? You can't do that!'

'But I'm in pain . . .'

Her eyebrows bedded themselves down in lines which pointed angrily towards her nose.

'You are Somalian, just like me,' she said. 'If you do that it will have massive consequences for you. I don't want to be responsible for you being opened! I won't tell the doctor that. You will be talked about, your mother will be devastated and your family dishonoured – people will call you a whore, no one will marry you . . .'

For a minute, all I could do was stare at her. I couldn't believe the words that were tumbling from her mouth. We were thousands of miles away from Somalia, in another culture. This couldn't be happening! This white woman wanted to help me and the translator wouldn't tell her how. The doctor sat behind her desk and watched, her eyes flicking between the pair of us, obviously trying to understand what was being said.

'I don't care who marries me or doesn't marry me,' I said firmly. 'I don't care what Somalian people think. I want to be opened. Can you please tell the doctor what I want? That is your job.'

She point-blank refused. '*Mayo*,' she said – no.

I tried again. Again she refused.

'*Mayo*. I'm not going to be responsible for you destroying your life.'

'I'm not destroying my life,' I told her. 'I'm trying to build it. And you need to tell her I want to be opened.'

She shook her head, and wagged her finger at me. '*Mayo, mayo, mayo.*'

The doctor was leaning across her desk at this point, I assume asking the translator to repeat in English what I was saying, but the translator just sat there shaking her head.

'Who the hell are you to refuse to translate for me?' I said suddenly, frustration now bubbling over into anger. 'You are not my auntie. We might be Somalian but I don't know you. You're an evil woman. Just do what you're paid to do!'

And again she said no.

'Burn in hell,' I spat out at her. And at this point, the doctor stood up from behind her desk. She'd obviously seen enough. She led me to her door, and gestured for me to sit outside. The door closed and I heard them arguing behind it – I think everybody in the waiting room did. I longed to know what was being said, but a few moments later, when the translator left the room, slamming the door behind her and opening her mouth to give me one last lecture, I had an inkling.

I put my hand up to silence her. 'Bye bye,' I said. And she was gone.

When I went back into the office, it was clear that the doctor now knew what I wanted, and gave me an appointment to go to a different surgery a few days later. I was going to be opened. I knew that for certain.

As arranged, I attended a different surgery to undergo the procedure. I was taken into the room where I'd be operated on and I noticed a shaped knife, a needle and an apron. The smell of antiseptic permeated the room, the sterilised tools glinted in their packaging, and rolls of gauze were stacked neatly nearby. How different from the crude tools used to inflict this mutilation upon me.

I undressed as the doctor instructed, and lay upon the couch. She showed me the needle and did her best to explain that she was going to numb the area. All these surgical objects seemed so alien, and yet, despite how terrifying it felt to expose myself again, to open my legs so she could do her work, the equipment she held up looked so clean, everything was so professional, so calm, compared to what I'd experienced before. This time I was in control, I was deciding what happened to my body, so there was no need to be scared; I just had to listen to what she said, try to understand, and let her help me. There was no translator this time, perhaps because of what had occurred before.

The sharp prick of the needle as the anaesthetic was injected into my skin was nothing compared to the pain I'd known all those years ago. There was a flowery curtain that separated the couch I was on from the rest of the room, and so as she got to work, I focused on that, until a few minutes later the doctor looked up and indicated that it was done. She had opened me, just as I'd wanted, not all the way, just an inch or so, but enough to expose my urethra so I could wee properly.

As I lay there, a part of me hoped that the process of being opened would undo all of the damage – that somehow it might give me back the life I'd had before I was cut, and that it might magically restore my relationship with my mother. As if by repairing what had been done to me physically, I could wipe away the psychological scars too.

I rested on the doctor's couch for over an hour after the surgery, waiting and recovering. Every so often she checked on me, making sure I wasn't in any pain, asking if I was OK and receiving my nod in reply. And then finally I asked to go to the toilet.

Once the doctor had helped me down from the bed, I hobbled to the cubicle, pulled the string to turn on the light and shut the door behind me. Carefully I lifted my gown and slowly lowered myself on to the toilet. And there, in that tiny room, I weed normally for the first time in twelve years. Out it came, in one great gush, a full flow at last. And suddenly, my mind took me back to being six years old, of dashing in and out of the toilet as I had as a child, my mother chastising me for being too quick. 'Go back in there and wash your hands!' I heard her saying, and I smiled then because I'd been given back a happy memory of a better time. For a second, I had my Hoyo back, and then she was gone. I let out a huge sigh, and several great sobs, as I sat on that plastic toilet seat and felt a release that was both physical and emotional. I was one more step closer to freedom.

8

Yusuf

The man who came to pick us up from Leyton station was tall, slim, with a huge smile. His name was Yusuf, and this was to be the first time I clapped eyes on my future husband. Not that I knew it at the time. Nasra and Habiba had been talking about us getting a place of our own for a few weeks now. Three months had rolled by in the hostel, queuing up for our breakfast each morning and paying £1.70 for an evening meal. We got used to the rules of the place, that we had to be in before 10pm or we'd be locked out by Melanie, who guarded the front door. Nasra said a place of our own would give us more freedom; we'd be able to cook together, come and go as we pleased.

Margaret offered to help me fill in the forms for housing benefit, and Nasra had heard of some other girls who had found their own place. They'd had help from some Somalian guys who knew an estate agent in Leyton, east London, so Nasra said she'd go and meet them for us, to find out if we could do it too. She arrived home that evening, not full of news about the house, but of Yusuf, and when I saw him arrive at the station I felt heat race to my cheeks because I understood why.

Yusuf was also to be the first Somalian man I'd ever spoken to without being chaperoned by my mother or an auntie. I had, after all, been warned that speaking to men would give me a bad name, so even though I was miles from Somalia and its dusty streets, I was glad to have the other girls from the hostel there with me. Each Friday when I called my mother, it was always the first question she asked: 'Have you been talking to any boys?'

Yusuf took us to the house he shared with two other Somalian men, which was just five minutes from the station along ordinary suburban streets where life peeped out from net curtains behind each window. We went up to his room on a morning that was full of firsts for me. I had never so much as been alone with a man before and now I was in a man's bedroom. The room was very basic, and I told myself he had it set up more like a sitting room anyway. A single bed was pushed up against the wall; there was a TV and a prayer mat at the foot of his bed. But even the intimacy of knowing that was where he slept made me feel nervous. The other girls must have noticed how I was drinking in every detail.

Yusuf was up and down the stairs bringing us tea.

'Who's making this tea for him?' I whispered to Nasra as he left to go and get us some biscuits.

'Yusuf is,' she said.

'Wow. He knows how to make tea?'

'Of course!' she laughed at me.

I knew that I sounded stupid even to other Somalian girls, but they had been in Europe longer than me. They had made friends, they had got used to the sights and sounds, and I was so naive compared to them. All I knew was that this wasn't typical of any of the Somalian men I'd known back at home, the uncles who drifted in and out of their kitchen, expecting the women would make their food, or the male cousins who weren't required to clear the table or clean the pots and pans like we girls were after we'd eaten. Where I came from men were waited on – none who visited our villa would ever have dreamt of making tea. This man was obviously different, and I found him intriguing from that moment onwards. Not that I thought of him in that way, he was Nasra's friend, and it was clear from the way that she talked about him – dropping his name into conversations, giggling when he picked us up from the station – that she hoped for more from their relationship.

He appeared at the door again.

'I'm going to have lunch soon – shall I make some for all of us?'

While the other girls nodded in appreciation, I looked up at him dumbfounded.

'You cook?' I said, failing in any attempt to hide the surprise in my voice.

'Of course!' he replied, that wide grin of his seeming to fill the whole doorframe. And off he disappeared again downstairs. Sitting

CUT

there with the girls, I couldn't stop thinking about this man. He makes tea, he can cook? I had to see this for myself.

I made an excuse that I needed to go to the toilet and then wandered down the stairs, following the smells into the kitchen. And there he was.

'I was just looking for . . . You know how to chop onions?' I said, as I watched him carefully slice the flesh of the pale vegetables with precise, tiny movements.

He looked up then. 'I'm making pasta.'

'You are chopping onions?!' I said again.

He laughed then. 'What's wrong with that?'

'How long have you been chopping onions?' I asked him. 'Doesn't it hurt your eyes?'

He laughed once more, and that smile of his caught my attention again.

'Sit down,' he said. 'Let me tell you about onions.'

I sat down on a chair as he told me about all the other Somalian recipes he could cook and we laughed together.

Nasra must have heard me giggling from upstairs because suddenly she was at my side with a look on her face that instantly silenced me.

'What are you doing?' Nasra said.

'She's obsessed with onions,' Yusuf said. And I smiled at him, knowing then that our moment was over.

I left them in the kitchen, but even in the bathroom I found myself still giggling. What was this strange feeling, like thousands of butterflies fluttering deep inside my tummy and making my heart quicken to keep up with the beat of their wings? I remembered Nasra, and instantly felt guilty, so I was determined to put all thoughts of him out of my mind. We spent the afternoon at his house, talking about our plans, and Yusuf offered to speak to an estate agent and help us find a house to rent. He walked us back to the station, through streets I recognised from the journey to his place, past green bins tucked away behind short garden walls, past cats that looked out from their pretty pathways, across roads and down side streets. All the time I walked behind him, I could only think of that smile that had its back to me.

At the station I watched as Yusuf hugged each girl goodbye and the anxiety grew as he got closer to me. Immediately, and riddled with more guilt, I thought of my mother thousands of miles away. What would she say if she could see me hugging a man in the—, but before I had finished that sentence in my head, he'd already wrapped his huge arms around me. I returned his embrace with a brief, awkward hug and then dropped my arms as my face burned with embarrassment.

As we parted ways I turned to the girls and asked, 'Is it normal to hug men in the street?'

'Oh Hibo!' they said, and their laughter rang out across the train tracks.

That, of course, was not the last time I saw Yusuf, because he turned up at our hostel the next day. Not to see Nasra, but to see me. Despite the fact that I'd thought of nothing but him since we'd met, when I saw him standing there on the front steps I panicked.

'Hello, Hibo,' he said, that smile there with him on the doorstep.

'Nasra's not here,' I said.

'It's not Nasra that I've come to see ... It's you.'

I slammed the door shut almost before the words had finished leaving his mouth.

I stood behind the door, my heart pounding. Me? He'd come to see me?

Slowly I opened the door again; he was there on the other side of it, smiling, unfazed.

'What do you mean you've come to see me?' I said.

'I like you. I'd like to talk with you.'

This time I slammed the door so quickly it rattled within the doorframe. And yet the draw of him on the other side was too hard to resist.

'OK, what do you want to talk about?' I said, opening the door again, hesitantly.

'Let's go to that coffee shop across the road,' he said, pointing and laughing, undeterred by my brusque manner.

'One coffee,' I said, pointing my finger so he could count.

I grabbed my coat and we walked across the street. I was aware of him at my side, and when our jackets brushed together, I took another step away. But more than that I was aware of my heart fluttering in my chest; he wanted to talk and yet I was afraid the fear might steal my words. In the cafe, he ordered me a coffee and we sat down. My face was set like stone; I could only hope he wouldn't notice that my hand was shaking as I stirred sugar into my hot drink.

'Well, you wanted to talk, so talk,' I said abruptly.

And he did, he told me all about himself, where he was from in Somalia, how he'd left there when he was eighteen and had gone to Egypt, how he'd slept rough in the parks there, and even how he'd fallen in love with a woman there but her parents wouldn't allow them to marry. The thought of this made me feel a little sick. I wasn't sure why – after all, we were only having coffee. Even though I was fascinated by every little detail I tried my best to appear as if I wasn't interested in the least.

'Now tell me about you,' he said.

'What do you want to know?'

'Everything.'

And so I did. I told him about our house back in Mogadishu, about my mother, my aunties, my cousins, about Kenya, about London. And unlike me, he smiled and laughed and raised his eyebrows, just as interested in every single part of my story as I'd been in his, only he dared to show it.

'I'd like to see you again,' he said, once we'd drunk down the last of our coffees.

'Why?' I said. 'It's Nasra who likes you and she's my friend.'

'But I like you,' he said. 'Nasra is more like a sister to me.'

And it was all I could do not to trip over the tables and chairs I was so desperate to leave that cafe, because, of course, I liked him too.

That night in the hostel, I couldn't contain myself. I was skipping and jumping around the kitchen like a little kid, humming songs and making jokes with the other girls. It was all I could do not to mention Yusuf's name, and then, it just came out. I couldn't resist the urge to talk about him, even if it was to Nasra.

'Yusuf came here today. I think he was looking for you.'

Nasra looked up. 'Did you speak to him?'

'No,' I lied. 'I just saw him out of the window.'

She looked at me as if she wasn't sure whether to believe me or not.

The following day, Nasra came to my room and told me that Yusuf had called her and told her he'd been to see me. She said all the right things, but I could tell from her eyes that she was a little hurt. The atmosphere between us was tense; I felt bad for my friend.

'It's OK,' she said. 'I saw the way that you looked at each other. Yusuf is a decent man, you're lucky; you should get to know him.'

I could see that she was trying to be happy for us.

'He said he likes you,' she said. 'He also told me you like him too.'

'What? How does he know I like him?' I said.

And then she dissolved into giggles because she had caught me out. For the first time in my life, I had to accept that I liked a man.

The next few months were spent walking the streets of London with Yusuf as pink buds started to open up on the trees, and the last of the dead leaves were blown away by a final wintery breeze. Soon shocks of golden daffodils burst from the ground and, if I'd thought London was beautiful in the winter, it was even more lovely in the spring. And I couldn't help thinking that Yusuf played his part in making it feel so special.

Yusuf

My sister had arrived in London during the time Yusuf and I were getting to know each other and my mother had insisted I left the hostel to move in with her. I tried to keep my relationship with Yusuf a secret, a guilty feeling washing over me each time I arrived home to Hadsan's suspicious face. Not that we so much as held hands! Instead, we walked and walked, getting to know the whole of London, sometimes talking about everything and nothing, sometimes strolling in a comfortable silence; but I noticed how tiny electric shocks shot through me if our arms so much as brushed against our thick winter coats.

'I want to hold your hand,' he'd told me one day as we walked along the Strand.

'Why do you want to do that?' I said. 'Just walk along beside me.'

By now Yusuf knew better than to accept my initial curt responses; he knew there was a soft centre inside and that I was scared. He could see that by the way I looked away shyly when he told me what beautiful hair I had, or how pretty my eyes were.

'I love the way your hair brushes your face,' he'd say. I saw in his eyes just how much he meant it, and even though his compliments made me wriggle with discomfort, at the same time I loved every single one of them. So one day, after about three months, when he stopped dead in the street and kissed me on my cheek, I'd returned it with a hug, and we decided there and then that we wanted to get married.

But first, there was something I needed to tell him, and I was frightened. I realised by now that I loved this man, but I also knew that my revelation might mean I'd lose him for good. I'd been brought up with the strong message that men only wanted women who'd been cut, and I still carried the physical scars of that message even though I had been opened. Would Yusuf be the kind of man who would understand about all this? Over the weeks I'd tried to find the courage to bring up the subject, but how could I? How could I talk about my vagina with a man who I wouldn't yet allow to hold my hand? I'd started, I'd tried, I'd said to him that there was something I needed to talk about. And then I'd closed down, too shy, too terrified, to explain any more. But if we were going to have a future together I knew I had to say something.

We were sitting in a cafe that day, him sipping at his espresso, me hugging my hot cappuccino. I asked if I could try his espresso, but he laughed and said I was hyper enough as it was.

'I need to talk seriously for a moment,' I told him, and I watched his face change, a mixture of curiosity and perhaps a little fear.

'I'm not like other Somalian women,' I explained.

'I know that . . .' he said, grinning at me.

'When I arrived in England, I went to a doctor and . . . well, I'm not "signed, sealed, delivered" . . .'

Yusuf looked confused.

I sighed before trying something else, but my own racing heart was distracting me from what I wanted to say.

'Remember how they mutilate girls in Somalia?' I said. 'How they sew us together?'

I saw the recognition flash across his face, and his expression became more serious as he listened.

'Well, I went to the doctor and got opened . . .'

And that's where I left it. It felt like I'd dropped a bomb between us, that I'd laid down on that table something so personal, so painful, that it could blow us apart. But I had to know how Yusuf felt because I could never let any girls of my own go through the same.

I scoured his face for some clue to his reaction and the only thing I could detect there was relief.

'My sisters went through *gudnin*,' he said, dipping his eyes to the floor. 'I saw how they suffered. Even on her wedding night, one of them nearly died.'

Just like me, he'd never been told this directly, but he'd heard the whispers about how she'd spent three months in hospital after her wedding night. That was enough to put him off cutting girls for life.

'I expected this from you, and if you hadn't already been opened, I would have taken you to the doctor's myself before we got married.'

The relief on my face must have mirrored his one hundredfold. This man, who surprised me from the moment I realised he made cups of tea and chopped onions, was also against girls being cut in the name of men. He had witnessed the results of the brutality his own sisters had been subjected to, and he knew it was wrong. It was as simple as that. But I had one more thing I needed to be sure of.

'If we have children, my girls will not be touched,' I told him. 'I can handle my family. Can you take the pressure from yours?'

He took my hand across the table and, as people passed by the windows outside, he looked into my eyes and told me very slowly.

'They will be my children,' he said. 'And no one is going to tell me what to do with them. Any girls who come along won't be touched. I promise you.'

And there in that cafe, as life and traffic rushed by, I took a further step towards freedom. After all the physical pain I had suffered, the emotional trauma I'd borne, the cultural stigmatism I had had to fight against, I had met a man with whom I could create a future, one that would be safe for my unborn daughters. Even though they didn't exist yet, it was the greatest gift of freedom I could give them.

Yusuf and I married a few days later.

9

Sex

Our wedding was not traditional in the way that you might imagine; there were no intricate patterns of henna painted on my hands, no *shash* placed upon my head by my mother. There were no elders to take me aside and explain to me what my new husband might expect from our marriage, or in the bedroom. But it didn't stop my mind taking me there and that dark thought made me shudder. Instead, our marriage was carried out in secret, a simple ceremony at a friend's house in Whitechapel; a sheikh came and made an engagement between us, the Koran bearing witness to our promise to one another rather than family and friends. The bride wore blue jeans and a blue jumper, because winter was biting at the single-glazed windows, as well as a slightly sad expression because this wasn't the seven-day festival I'd grown up with, not what I'd imagined for myself as a little girl. The groom also wore jeans and a blue shirt, and Yusuf's two friends took us for an Indian meal after the sheikh had sealed our promise to one another.

I didn't go home to my sister's house that night, although I gave her no explanation why; I hadn't told her that Yusuf and I were getting married because I knew she'd try to stop me. Instead, for the first time, I went home with my new husband. As I opened the door to his room my hands felt clammy, but my heart melted at the sight of the new peach bedsheets and the flowers that he'd put out for me.

'I wanted to make it special for you,' Yusuf said.

He sat me down on the bed and from a tiny box produced a thin silver band; it was simple yet beautiful, and it meant so much – an unbroken circle of our never-ending love. Gently, he slipped it on to my wedding-ring finger.

'One day you will have a proper wedding. I promise you,' he said, kissing me. I hugged my husband tight and, out of the corner of my eye, studied the new sheets that he'd taken such care to make up for me. For us. Because this bed that we were sitting on was to become the place that we would lie together, and that thought alone took me back to my childhood bedroom, to Fatima telling me the only thing I'd ever heard about what it was to be married – that your husband is the rolling pin. I let go of Yusuf then for fear that he might feel the thudding inside my chest. I loved him, I wanted so desperately to be married to him, to be his wife in every sense of the word, but ever since we'd decided to make our union official nightmares about making love had crept into my sleep.

Sex

'Let's have some tea,' I said.

And that was the start of our married life. Not, like most couples, hours lost entwined within each other's arms and legs. Instead, I avoided that intimacy, jumping each time he came near me, or rubbed my arm, or kissed me, in case he wanted me to lie down next to him. And then I'd close my eyes and my breathing became that bit harder because, as much as I wanted to be everything to my new husband, I just couldn't stand even the thought of sex with him.

Yusuf must have sensed my fear.

'We don't have to do anything,' he said. 'We can just lie down next to each other; we don't even need to touch.'

So that's what we did the first night we spent together, me lying awake in the darkness, feeling the heat of him beside me, listening to the slow, steady sound of his breathing.

Then, in the morning, Yusuf's phone rang. It was Hadsan. He answered it, his face betraying none of the fear that was undoubtedly etched across mine.

'Hibo's right here with me . . .

'. . . We're not living in sin . . .

'. . . We're married.'

I didn't speak to Hadsan, but I could hear the fury in her voice from the other side of the room. She must have called my mother because when the phone rang again, it was Hadsan insisting I call Hoyo in Kenya. But I didn't, not then, not for days. I may not have been ready to experience everything marriage had to offer me, but for now it was a cocoon, a safe place for me.

That's where I stayed for days before speaking to my mother, protected by my husband's arms – nothing more, nothing intimate, and Yusuf never asked more from me. Each morning I'd jump out of bed to shower, ready for a new day of being his wife, but as the sky started to darken from afternoon into evening, the fear would seep into my bones; the terrifying thought that he might want to attempt to make love to me that night. Often it would turn me from a loving wife into one who was cold and aloof.

'What's wrong, Hibo?' he might ask, trying to pull me into a hug as I watched the TV.

'Nothing,' I'd say, shaking him off, my eyes pinned to the screen.

I tried to ignore the disappointment I'd spot in his eyes because it made me feel guilty that I wasn't prepared to make my husband happy in the traditional way that other wives do. But I knew I couldn't keep avoiding my husband forever.

Four days after our wedding, I finally spoke to my mother. The conversation went as I predicted it would.

'How could you?' she yelled down the phone. 'How could you do this without discussing it with anyone?'

'I did discuss it with someone,' I said, after I'd finished holding the receiver away from my ear. 'I discussed it with my husband.'

Yusuf winced on my behalf from the other side of the room as she ranted down the line. Eventually, when I realised she wouldn't let me speak, I hung up, and Yusuf held me in a big, strong hug.

My husband couldn't have been more gentle and support- ive in those first few days and weeks of marriage, and I wanted desperately to be the wife to him that he deserved, and so very carefully, I let him inch closer to me in bed, to hold my hand under the covers, to let his hand stray further over to my body.

There were many false starts when my heart would tell me that I was ready to make love to Yusuf, and then as he loomed over me, all I would see in my mind's eye was the cutter, and all I would feel was the pain, and panic would creep up my throat and strangle me from the inside. I'd cover my face and cry 'no'.

'Stop!' I'd say and he'd back off immediately, scooping me up in his arms.

'We don't have to do anything,' he'd say. 'I don't mind if we never make love.'

I wished that would make me feel better, that it would ease the pressure as he obviously hoped it might, but it didn't, it only left me riddled with guilt. So the next night we tried again, and the next, and the next. The nights turned into weeks and the weeks turned into months; and then finally, I allowed Yusuf into me, we consummated our marriage, and the pain was everything I thought it would be. I forced myself to bat away the images that flooded my mind. I closed my eyes and squeezed away the tears, and I tried instead to focus only on my husband's pleasure. But how could that be satisfying for either of us?

'Are you OK?' Yusuf asked me afterwards.

And a nod was all I could muster because even his gentle nature, his care and attention, were a reminder to me that I wasn't a whole woman, that I couldn't satisfy him or be satisfied in the same way as a woman who hadn't been cut. I'd heard gossip in our community about Somalian men leaving wives who couldn't satisfy them, and so in those disappointing early days I was plagued by such thoughts as I lay there with my husband in what should have been post-coital bliss.

Making love served only as a painful reminder that there was something missing from me that even Yusuf's love couldn't replace.

10

Forgiveness

The smile that stretched across Yusuf's face seemed to include far more teeth than it usually did, or perhaps I'd just never seen him smile quite so much. Yet at the same time, my own face was lined with worry. The source of our conflicting emotions lay buried deep inside my belly, a tiny bean of a thing that was busy growing arms and legs and a little nose while I went about my day. Our first child. Not that I wasn't happy about it, far from it. Since the first feelings of nausea and the early signs of my swelling stomach, I'd been delighted at the thought of this tiny person we'd created growing in there, safe and sound. Delighted and worried. Because it meant I was going from wife to mother and I didn't know if I could do it.

I hadn't told Yusuf straight away, I hadn't told anyone. For weeks

I disguised the sickness that took hold of me every day, stripping pounds of weight off me. I ignored the fact that I hadn't had a period for months, and refused to go to the doctor even when Yusuf guessed what was wrong.

'How will I know how to be a mother?' I'd ask in the darkness, as we lay in bed alongside each other.

'You will know,' Yusuf would answer, taking my hand under the sheets. 'You will be wonderful.'

I would wish then that I could be as sure. What kind of role model did I have to learn from, after all? What happy memories of my own childhood could I draw from that would tell me how to love my own child, given the betrayal I had suffered at the hands of my mother, and the distance that had existed between us ever since? Her kind of parenting was not the sort I wanted the new life growing inside me to have.

This evening, as if reading my mind, Yusuf gave my hand a squeeze and told me again: 'You will be fine, and we will look after our baby together – boy or girl. As long as it is healthy, that's all that matters.' And I prayed again in the darkness to keep our child safe until it was in my arms.

As I heard Yusuf's breathing descend into a heavy rumble, I lay there blinking out at the black and wondering how on earth I'd be a mum. And not any mum, a good mum. How would I know if my baby was happy? Would I know how to comfort it when it cried? Could I do this, could I love this child as much as I wanted to when the love that my mother had shown me had also known its limits? And when it came to the birth, how would I ever let a doctor look at me down there to deliver my baby? Yusuf and I had been married for three months by the time I had allowed him to penetrate me. After that the trust had built up and I'd allowed him to look at me between my legs.

'You look normal to me,' he'd insisted.

I'd uncovered my face from my hands and looked into his eyes for the reassurance I so desperately needed, and there it was, I could see it, but even that wasn't enough to convince me. So how would I let a stranger look, even if they were going to deliver my baby?

The child inside my belly was undeterred by my fears, though – it was determined to let me know it was coming whether I was ready or not. The following day, as I took a bath, it gave me a kick that sent ripples through the soapy water.

'Yusuf!' I cried, wide-eyed and curious about this little person growing within.

He burst into the bathroom thinking I'd fallen over, and when instead he'd found me safe and sound and I'd taken his hand and placed it on my warm skin, he beamed.

'That's our baby,' he said.

We were still living in the house Yusuf shared with two friends, but we knew that, with the baby coming, we'd need to get a place of our own. But one thing at a time; first we needed to have the scan.

A few days later we went to the hospital, and the first scan revealed I was a lot further along in my pregnancy than we had first thought. In fact, I was eighteen weeks, that's why I'd felt that little kick. The sonographer squirted cold jelly on to my belly and showed me arms and legs, ears, nose and eyes. She was even able to tell us that we were expecting a boy.

As Yusuf chatted away to her, I stared at the image and felt hot, fat tears rolling down my cheeks, because right there, on that screen, everything became real to me. The life inside me already needed me to be a mum, and in that instant I saw the future, rather than the past, and I knew that to move forward into it I needed to forgive my own mother. I needed to be filled with love, not anger; with tenderness, not bitterness. I needed to put down this sack of resentment that I'd carried around with me since I was cut, the one that weighed so heavily on my shoulders, and I needed to embrace this new start.

After that day, I revelled in the changes I could see happening to my body. I rubbed my tummy and wondered: had my mother done the same when I was growing inside her? How would she not have felt the same love swell inside her with each passing day? Somehow, knowing we'd shared this experience brought me closer to her than I had felt in years. She became human to me again.

Yet, in equal measure, I felt confused; as my own maternal instinct grew, I wondered again how she'd been able to turn away from me when I'd needed her most.

I tried to shake those thoughts right out of my head, though. 'The future, not the past, Hibo,' I reminded myself. But it was difficult to keep telling myself that when the past was always here, a part of my body, and that's what I dreaded the most, the past coming back to haunt me when medical staff needed to examine me. I'd escaped any kind of examination during my pregnancy, and my biggest fear was that doctors and midwives would think I was a freak, that they wouldn't regard me as a human being because of the mutilation that I had undergone. I couldn't look at myself, so how could they?

And then finally, after nine long months, came the first pain from deep inside, a sharp pain. Not that I told Yusuf, not even when I felt wet between my legs. Instead, I locked myself in the bathroom as the pains grew stronger and swept through me in waves, but I was more troubled by the anxious thoughts racing around my head: how is this baby going to come out? How will I deliver him if I won't – I can't – open my legs to anyone? What are they going to do? Am I going to die? Is this baby going to die? But even worse than any of that, the idea of myself or my baby dying, was the thought of medical staff looking between my legs – that's how huge my fear was.

But by midnight, my pains were so strong that there was no disguising them anymore, and, as soon as Yusuf realised, he insisted we go straight to the hospital. There, a midwife felt my stomach and attached a monitor to check the baby's heart rate.

'How long have you been having contractions?'

My English wasn't very good; I spoke only a few words, so Yusuf translated the bits that I didn't know.

'Not long,' I lied.

She studied me for a second.

'I'd like to examine you down below,' she said.

'No.'

She tried again. 'I need to know how dilated you are.'

'No.'

'Please, Hibo,' Yusuf begged me. 'Think of our baby.'

But I shook my head.

The midwife left and went to get a doctor. She came back and said it was fine, they would continue checking the baby's heart rate through the monitor. But she had a warning that Yusuf tried his best to translate.

'You have been carrying this baby for nine months; you don't want anything happening to him because you refuse to be checked.'

But then nature took over. They kept me in overnight and by 5am my contractions were stronger than ever; the baby was coming and I didn't have a choice in the matter. But even as my baby started to make his way through my body, as the doctors insisted I had to let my knees fall open to allow him to come out, my fear of their judgement still made me cover my face with a pillow and burst into tears because the images in my mind were not of the baby that was about to be born, but quick flashes of the cutter, my mother, the bag of rusty razors.

'We need to cut her,' the doctor told Yusuf. I needed an episiotomy so that my son could come out, the third time someone had taken a blade to my genitals, the second time it had been done without anaesthetic. The instant I saw the scalpel I was back there in that hut – only this time it wasn't my life I was fighting for, but my son's. I had to dig deep and push those images out of my head along with my son out of my body, so I took a deep breath but I couldn't stop the tears because I realised then that everyone in this hospital would know about me now, they knew what I looked like; that although that doctor had opened me so I could urinate, it was just a few centimetres, not entirely. There was no translator there, but I knew that the midwives were talking about me, not to me, *about* me. I just wanted to get away. *Please God*, I prayed, *just let it be over.*

Just to make things even more horrifying, Yusuf was looking over my shoulder, between my legs.

'He's coming!' he said. 'I can see his head! Keep pushing, Hibo!'

Then suddenly, a cry pierced the air. My son. And it is true that in that instant you forget everything. All the pain suddenly evaporated; he was something I could concentrate on instead of the faces of those around me. In that one second, he became my world, ten little fingers and ten little toes, he was perfect. We called him Abdinasir.

I'd suffered far more than I'd realised I would – having been stitched so tightly by the cutter, and crisscrossed with scar tissue, both of our lives had been endangered.

The stitching that was needed to put me back together took months to heal, and the pain made it impossible for me to sleep. Each time I closed my eyes I was that six-year-old child again, looking up at the tiny gap in the canvas. But in those dark nights when I couldn't sleep, I'd look over into Abdinasir's cot and watch him sleeping, and remind myself again: the future, not the past, Hibo.

Because there was the future, swaddled in blankets, sleeping peacefully. The pain would eventually go, the memories would fade again, and he'd still be here, the son who had given me life. My love for him overwhelmed everything else, the joy at holding him to my breast as I fed him overshadowing the past.

It was only after Abdinasir's birth that three letters appeared on my maternity files: FGM. I had no idea what those letters stood for, no one had explained them to me, yet instinct told me that everything I wanted to know, everything my mother hadn't told me, would be explained in those three letters. If I could just find out what they meant.

As soon as I was well enough to go out after the birth of my son, I put Abdinasir into his pram and wrapped him up in thick blankets. Our destination wasn't far as the wheels of the pram crunched through the last of the snow on the ground. In the months that I'd spent convalescing since the birth, in between the sleepless nights, the nappy changes and breastfeeds illuminated only by the moon that shone in through the bedroom curtains, those three letters kept going round in my mind. They had to have something to do with being cut.

I'd asked Yusuf to go to the library for me while I was busy with the baby, but each time he'd returned without any luck. 'I couldn't find anything,' he said, looking as frustrated as I felt. So I knew I needed to go myself, and luckily the library was just across from the new flat in Leyton we'd moved into in preparation for the birth of our son. But where to start among the endless rows of shelves? My grasp of the English language still stretched little past a hundred words, nothing like the vocabulary I'd need to skim the titles of hundreds of books. So I decided to start from the beginning. My son was just six months old, but I'd start teaching him English words as I learned myself. We sat there for hours, surrounded by the colourful spines of children's books and bright murals on the walls, as I held a picture book just inches from him in his pram. In this part of the library, it was usual for the silence to be broken by toddlers clambering up and down from chairs as they thrust another book into their mother's lap.

'Banana!' I'd say, showing Abdinasir a picture of a bright-yellow fruit, and he'd gurgle his appreciation as the letters made more sense to me in turn.

'Apple,' I'd turn the page. 'Orange.' His legs kicked happily inside his Baby-gro.

And like that, the pair of us learned English from children's books, until one day I was ready to ask the librarian for a Somali–English dictionary. Then my search really began. Wheeling Abdinasir's pram through the towering aisles, I found a section that looked like it covered medicine though the sheer number of books was daunting. Carefully, one hand rocking Abdinasir as he slept in his pram, the other running a finger along each spine, I found a book that had the words 'female circumcision' in the title. I knew what 'female' meant, and I tried the next word out loud, my tongue tangling itself around those new syllables. An 'f' and a 'c' in the title ... No 'g', but instinct told me this could be what I was looking for.

I took it down from the shelf and checked it out of the library, tucking it into the bag that I had slung over the handles of the buggy. At home, as I fed Abdinasir spoonfuls of puréed banana while he sat gurgling in his high chair, I flicked through the pages. And there, I found my answer. It was pictures rather than words that did the talking at first. They were just line drawings, but the shock of them was enough for me to snap the book shut.

So that is what I looked like.

Yusuf looked up from the television, startled by the unexpected sound. 'Is everything OK, my love?' he asked.

'This is what I've been looking for,' I told him, and the tears started flowing, even though I didn't yet understand a single word. He got up and came over to comfort me, briefly picking up the book and turning it over in his hands before returning it gently to the table.

For almost a year I kept that book at home, renewing it every few weeks. Each evening, after I'd put Abdinasir down to sleep, my finger traced every word on the page, flipping between the English word and the Somali translation in my dictionary, rearranging the words in the sentence until each one dropped into place, their meaning sinking in, often accompanied by devastation and reality. Every so often I'd look up at Yusuf and tell him something that I'd learned. He'd just listen – he knew I didn't need any comment from him, only an ear as I tried out these new words.

Then, as I made my way through one section, I came across those three letters. FGM: 'female genital mutilation'. I quickly scanned through my Somali–English dictionary for the translation of mutilation, and then I sank back in my chair. Mutilation. That's *exactly* what had happened to me. I couldn't think of a better word to describe it.

I closed my eyes and thought of the times my hand had strayed to that area as I'd bent down to wash myself in the bath or the shower. My fingers had felt none of the fleshy female parts that I'd seen pictures of in the other medical books I'd looked through during my search of the library – none of the normal pieces that make up a woman. Instead, the picture that my hands had created in my mind matched some of the images in this book. They were labelled in 'types', with a description of the extent of mutilation in each case – Type 1, Type 2, Type 3. This last one was the most brutal of all, and that's what had been done to me.

I put my hand up to my mouth as the simple line drawing settled itself into my brain. What had they done to me? Suddenly I felt curious about how I did look, what that doctor had seen when she opened me, what all the midwives saw at the hospital.

More than that, every page of this book, however painful each revelation I translated was, told me I wasn't alone. Each tear that splashed on to the page was being shed by another woman some-where else in the world.

I read about girls in Mali, in Nigeria, in Egypt, all of them had gone through this same mutilation. Although it helped in some ways to realise that other women knew my pain, it made me feel overwhelmingly sad. And again I came back to the question of why.

Over the next few weeks I read further. One eight-year-old Malian girl had told the author how she had been showered in gifts by her family and friends, and had been told by her mother that she was going to be brave and courageous and that this was a rite of passage that would make her into a real woman. I thought back to my own *gudnin*, the same lies – even the same words – had been told to me. There were tens of thousands of us girls all around the world who'd been tricked by their parents. Who thought that there was some reward at the end of being pinned down in a hut and having bits stripped off them, when in reality there was nothing but nightmare flashbacks and a lifetime of infections and pain.

I read on, translating slowly more words that revealed FGM was to blame for my constant urine infections, for the dryness I suffered, the scar tissue, the constant itching, the damaged nerve endings, and was the reason I felt no sensation of pleasure when Yusuf made love to me.

As I read each woman's testimony, it was like reading my own. I knew then that I truly wasn't alone, and nor was I alone in my need for knowledge. Someone had taken the time to ask more questions than I ever had – they'd asked and had answered so many whys that there was enough information to fill a whole book. That made me feel that what happened to me had some meaning for other people too. That it shouldn't have happened. I realised that this thing that has haunted me since I was a child wasn't a secret at all. You *could* talk about it, if only someone was willing to listen. I didn't feel so alone anymore, but at the same time I began to be haunted by the idea that there were girls being cut outside of my community, outside of Mogadishu, all around the world, maybe even here in Britain – it was that thought which kept me awake at night over the next few months, more than the cries of my teething baby.

By the time I finished reading the book, I knew I needed to see how I looked. Pictures in books weren't enough – I wanted to see for myself what that cutter had done to *me*. I was frightened, more than I can ever write here on these pages. I wasn't ready to position myself awkwardly over a mirror; I didn't want to be alone with the shock of what I might find in my reflection, and I wasn't ready to share that moment with Yusuf. I wanted a degree of separation, the chance to shut my eyes; the images in the book were real enough without seeing a living, breathing me held up in front of the mirror. These were the days before smartphones and digital cameras, so the only thing I could think of was a disposable camera from my local pharmacy. I bought one a few days later, throwing it into Abdinasir's changing bag like a dirty secret. Then, in the privacy of my bathroom while Yusuf was out at work and Abdinasir slept, I climbed into an empty bathtub and opened my legs, looking away as I positioned the camera between them. Click. Click. Click. With shaking hands I wound the film between each shot.

For days I eyed the small black plastic box – it looked so ordinary and innocuous, sitting there in our living room on the shelf above our TV. I knew the weight of what it contained within, though: indelible images already burnt on to the film. Did I have the courage to get them out?

A week later, I went back to the pharmacy, and there I spoke to the female assistant standing behind the counter. She must have been in her thirties, covered, like me, in a *hijab*. I took that as a sign that she might understand what I needed to explain to her.

'I have something really private in here that I need to see,' I told her in my broken English.

Her brow wrinkled slightly.

'They are pictures of me that I have never seen before,' I continued, and pointedly directed my eyes downwards.

Her brow ironed itself out again, as a flicker of recognition of what I was trying to say crossed her face. She took the camera.

'I understand,' she said, speaking partly in English, partly in Arabic, which she guessed I might know. 'I will look after it personally.'

The look that we shared between us told me that I could trust her, and as I left the pharmacy there was a sense of relief mixed in with the other feelings of fear and trepidation.

I returned to the pharmacy the following week, and as soon as the bell on the door jangled to signal my arrival, she was instantly at my side to tell me the photographs were ready.

'Did you look already?' I asked her.

She shook her head. 'Did you want me to?'

I nodded. I don't know why, but something told me that I didn't want to do this on my own.

As if reading my thoughts she said gently, 'I have a friend who this happened to. I know what you're afraid of seeing.'

'Will you look for me first?' I asked her, and she nodded.

She pointed to a plastic seat in the corner in front of the counter, and I sat down and waited as she went to look in a private room. When she came out, I was sure that her skin was a shade paler.

'What do I look like?' I asked her. 'Tell me honestly.'

'It is devastating,' she warned, and I saw her eyes were shining with tears.

My heart was racing and my hands were covered in a film of sweat as she led me to the back room.

'You can stay here for as long as you need to,' she said, closing the door behind her.

It took me a long while to look. I sat there, turning the packet over and over in my hands, sometimes starting to open it before sealing it again. By the time I'd finished, the lip of the envelope curled with its own curiosity, and so before the clock could tick another hand around, I pulled the pile of photographs from the envelope at last. What I saw took the breath from my body. The woman was right, there was only one word for it: devastating.

For the first time I could see what I had been left with. It was just a hole. Everything else had been chopped off and sealed up. Despite the doctor opening my skin enough to expose my urethra so I could wee, there were no fleshy labia like other women had, no protection, no beauty. The area between my legs looked like dark-brown sand that someone had dragged a faint line through. Then, as if someone had poked a stick into the sand, there at the bottom of the line was a hole. My vagina. I could see it was a little bigger than how it had originally been stitched thanks to the doctor who opened me slightly, but there it was, the only clue that I was a woman. The rest of my genitals had been sliced off and discarded, yet my urethra was just visible where the doctor had partially deinfibulated me during that minor surgery.

I wiped the tears from my face with my scarf, preparing to leave the room. I don't know what I had hoped for by seeing myself – to reclaim some sense of ownership over my body perhaps? To see my body mutilated like that, to grasp for the first time what the result of all that unbearable pain had been, to know why I had suffered in childbirth and every day since – it was truly devastating. No other word.

'Please dispose of them,' I asked the assistant as I left the shop.

I didn't of course see the photos again, yet the horror of those images was seared on my mind. But did I wish I'd never looked? No. I just saw it as the next painful step on the path to freedom, because I knew then – and I'd always known – that knowledge is power.

11

Family

I might have discovered what FGM meant, but it was still not discussed with me by any midwife, not even the one who picked up the notes to my second pregnancy two years after Abdinasir's birth. By now my English was much better; I would have talked had there been anyone prepared to listen. But nobody mentioned it and so I didn't either. This was still the early nineties, and despite the influx of Somalian refugees – which told me that surely I couldn't be the only woman they had seen who had undergone such a horrific procedure – it was a subject not talked about openly, even by medical professionals on this side of the world, a supposedly more civilised place, thousands of miles away from the shroud of secrecy surrounding the practice.

While making love to my husband remained something that I endured rather than enjoyed, I still wanted to be close to him in that way. I still tried not to deny him simply because I couldn't bear to see on his face the pain that I inflicted by rejecting him. We went to the doctor's together and our GP recommended a lubricant to make things easier, but although it took away some of the pain, it did little to combat the flashbacks that accompanied our time together in bed.

'Are you OK?' Yusuf would ask.

And I wished so much that he didn't need to ask me. I wished I was a normal woman.

By now, with a young baby, I mixed with more Somalian women in our community, and even though we all shared the pain of our circumcision, we never discussed it openly. We disguised it with humour, 'joking' about how we winced in bed. I look back now and wonder how we could have coped in that way, but you do what you can to get through these things in life. I heard stories time and time again of women who'd been left by their husbands, often because they had found another woman, and even if we didn't say it out loud, we all knew that the fact that we had been mutilated was to blame. Yusuf had always been such a wonderfully supportive husband, he'd never given me any reason to fear he would be anything but loyal to me, and yet I lived with the constant anxiety that I wouldn't be enough for him, that one day he might seek pleasure from a woman who could please him in that department. My fear became part of my everyday life, even as our family grew.

Family

During my second pregnancy it was a huge relief when doctors told me that I would be able to have a Caesarean this time around, seeing how I'd struggled so much during Abdinasir's birth. For me the prospect of not being exposed to any more strangers was enough to help me relax throughout the pregnancy. And yet when the time came to go into hospital, as I waddled in for my elective Caesarean, my belly full of arms and legs, and a drip was put into my back which sent my legs to sleep, I hadn't realised that they'd need to go down there to insert the catheter. As the nurse looked between my legs, I closed my eyes and tried to take myself away from the room, unsure of whether I really did spot horror flit across her face.

Our second son Ali's birth was much calmer than the first, but because I hadn't pushed my boy into the world, I felt that there was something missing from the experience, however traumatic my first labour had been. And then there were the horror stories I heard in the playground as Abdinasir toddled round my knees and I rocked Ali gently in his pram. Other Somalian women told how their friends had been unwittingly sterilised while undergoing Caesareans. I didn't know whether these were Chinese whispers, but they were enough to make me vow never to have another. So eighteen months later when my breasts swelled and my periods stopped, I told no one. My growing tummy was easy to disguise behind the weight that had been left over from my two previous pregnancies, and although Yusuf begged me to visit our GP, I refused.

I was six months pregnant by the time I went to hospital for my

117

first scan and my midwife was furious. But her disappointment in me did little to dampen the joy I felt when we discovered that this time we were having a baby girl. I loved my boys with all my heart, but having a girl meant something different to me; it meant that I could mend the past. My girl, after all, would never be cut, despite – or, more accurately, because of – being born to a mother whose life had been ruined by FGM. It was my vow; the cycle would be broken.

I would love her well past her sixth birthday; we would play together and talk together about anything and everything, and do all the things that my mother and I missed out on. I would buy her dolls and dress her up prettily and tell her stories, and she would never know the misery that I had felt in my childhood. She would never be let down by me like I was by my mother. I would raise her as a normal human being, with as much chance as any other person in this world, and she would never know the terror that I had met so early on in my life. This time, things would be different.

My hostility towards my mother continued to abate as I watched her become a loving grandmother. What she hadn't bestowed on me after the age of six, she gave to my sons tenfold. She had moved over to the UK a few months after Abdinasir had been born, and although she didn't accept my marriage to Yusuf, and refused to speak to him, she showered our boys in more love than I'd known she was capable of. They'd look for Granny out of the window of our flat when they knew she was coming to visit. They loved nothing more than the days she'd surprise them by coming with me to pick them up from school. Each Saturday I took them to my sister's house where my mother lived and she would take them out to the local market, returning them with arms bulging with sweets and toys. Slowly, we exchanged smiles, and then conversations, and then hugs. And time did soften how she felt about Yusuf too; in fact, the time came when she apologised to him for refusing to acknowledge him in my life.

'You are a good man, a good husband, and a good father,' she told him. 'And I am sorry.'

It was another step towards mending our shattered relationship.

But when our daughter Amal was born in 1996, we grew even closer. As was my wish, I delivered her naturally, and while it was just as painful as my first, I was more prepared for what to expect. Again, no one mentioned FGM to me; it was a knowing silence that pervaded the room, burst only by Amal's cries as I pushed her into the world.

She quickly grew into Daddy's little princess. She would wait at the window for him to come home from work, racing to open the door before his key even scratched its way into the lock. And wherever he'd been, he'd have picked up a little present for her, every single day without fail; a bracelet, a dress, a ring. She was a spoilt little girl, but Yusuf adored her. And so did my mother. Seeing her with Amal changed everything. My eldest daughter was a mirror image of me as a child – huge brown eyes, skinny legs and a curious mind to match. I saw the way my mother smothered her with affection and it took me back to how she'd been with me; watching them was like reliving my childhood. The love they shared wasn't just a gift for them, but for me too. It was like having my Hoyo back.

'She's so much like you, Hibo,' she would say, and a look would pass between us.

But it was inevitable, too, that sooner or later somebody would ask when she was going to be cut. If Yusuf's family questioned him on the telephone from Africa, he never told me, but it was my sister who first asked me when I was going to do it.

We were chatting in the kitchen, Amal playing at our feet, when Hadsan turned to me.

'You need to cut her while she's young so she doesn't remember,' she told me.

'She's never going to be cut,' I replied.

She looked at me, shocked, raising her eyebrows in surprise.

'What? Never?'

'Never,' I said.

'But . . .'

'I don't want to discuss it, but I'm not going to cut any of my girls. That's it.'

'But what about Yusuf? His family?'

'His family are not my concern. Yusuf believes as I do that our girls will never be cut.'

'Who is going to marry her if she's not cut?'

'Whoever she marries is her business.'

'You will change your mind one day,' she said, staring at me hard.

And I stared back at her thinking, *You are crazy if you think I'd put my girls through that.*

120

We moved from Leyton to Walthamstow a few years afterwards, into a lovely three-bedroom flat just a stone's throw from the busy market. It was the most space we'd ever had, and yet our love for our children meant that we only planned to fill it with more; in fact, by 2001, I was pregnant with another little girl, Aisha.

Right in the centre of Walthamstow there was a great community atmosphere; a whole mix of different cultures, not just other Somalian families. I wouldn't cook a meal without sending one of my children round with some food for our neighbours, and they would do the same for us, giving the kids sweets for Eid even if they didn't celebrate it themselves. With each pregnancy, I became less frightened of the birth itself and more excited to meet the new baby. Yusuf and I were happy and our family grew and the years passed, even though in the back of my mind there still lurked the anxiety that he might one day want a more fulfilling sex life – that one day he might grow tired of my wincing as we made love, of my reticence to initiate intimacy. I always tried to reassure him that if I didn't find some enjoyment from our love-making I wouldn't keep having his babies. For me, being close to him, the feeling of his skin on mine, was what I enjoyed.

But, like many people, our family life wasn't without its share of sadness. Just as I had begun to rebuild my relationship with my mother, age and the march of time took their toll on her frail body. She was living with my sister but often spent the day with us. I waved goodbye to her one day in particular, my hands resting on my belly which was bulging with my little girl as I watched Yusuf help her into the car to drive her home, and that would be the last time I saw my big and beautiful mother fit and well. An hour later I got a worried phone call.

'I'm at the hospital,' Yusuf told me. 'Your mother has had a stroke.'

In that second, my world fell to the floor. Yusuf was terrified what the upset might do to me in my heavily pregnant state; he begged me to stay away from the hospital. But too many years had been lost between Hoyo and me; I wasn't going to let the past get in the way of what little time we might have left. The stroke left Hoyo bedbound for four years and many of those were spent barely recognising me, let alone being aware of the birth of Aisha or even Abdilahi, two years later. My children missed her, and I did too. When my sister needed to go away on holiday for a few weeks, she asked me to care for Hoyo. I stayed with her for the whole time, carefully tracing a cold compress across her skin, talking to her, telling her stories about the children. I made her delicious soups, and fed them to her ever so gently with a spoon, just as she had once done for me. And slowly in those weeks, by some miracle, the paralysis left her, the mist lifted, and she could once again see me as her daughter. She lifted herself up in bed on her hands; she wanted to talk for the first time in years.

'I need you to forgive me, Hibo,' she said in a frail voice.

I knew instantly what she meant, but I needed to hear it. I moved closer so that she could see me better. I felt her breath against my face and I clasped her cheeks in the palms of my hands; her skin felt paper-thin and hung around her jaws where it had once been fleshy and plump. I remembered suddenly the mother who had pulled me on to her knees and fed me *anjero*; she was the same woman, nothing had changed, not when I looked into her deep-brown eyes.

'Forgive you for what?' I asked, one tear making its slow trail down my cheek.

'I know how you felt when you were cut,' she said. 'I know how it disturbed you.'

Even to hear her acknowledge my pain was enough to take the breath from inside me. I tried to find some words to reply but it felt like my heart had stolen them all.

'I forgave you a long time ago,' I said eventually.

'When?' she asked.

And I told her then about that first scan I'd had when I was pregnant with Abdinasir. 'If I hadn't forgiven you then, I knew I wouldn't be a good mum. I'm sorry I didn't tell you before.'

'Thank you, Hibo,' she said. 'God bless you.'

We both knew there hadn't been the chance to say this before, that we couldn't talk to each other about what had happened. If I closed my eyes I could still see the hut that had been erected in my honour; I could still smell the canvas that had been heated by the sun, and see the smoke that wound its way up out of the hole in the roof and into the stars above while the rest of the family ate and chattered in the house just yards away from me. But I also knew that it had been taken down a long time ago, that if I went back to that villa now, if I stood in the yard, I might still find the same trees, but there would be no place where I had lain. The hut had been dismantled, and we were here in Britain. We were free. The past was in the past and I was now a thirty-two-year-old mother of five, but I needed Hoyo to know that *gudnin* would have no place in my children's future. Even if it broke the spell of this precious moment. I needed her to know that I had a legacy of my own.

'You know my girls? They will never be cut.'

I waited for the reaction on her face, and there it was, undeniable disappointment sprang to her watery eyes. Now Hoyo knew that it ended with me, I wasn't going to repeat her mistake. Instead of feeling angry with her and my heart breaking all over again, I felt sorry for her. For the first time, in that bed, I saw a woman who had been cut just like me, another victim of this barbaric practice, but unlike me she hadn't been able to talk about it, read about it, or ask why. She had accepted being cut as her fate; she had believed her own mother who'd told her that she must be cut in order to remain pure. She didn't know or think to question what was being done to her; she had no idea that this modern world would see it for what it was – child abuse.

I felt sorry for my mother for being uneducated. I wondered how many millions of mothers had come before her – and since – who hadn't been able to express the pain they'd felt when their genitals were cut, when pieces of their flesh were sliced off them, all for the sake of a man. But I still couldn't rationalise how, as a grandmother, she still wanted my children to go through that pain – her cultural ties were more tightly knitted inside of her than her blood bond to my children. And that made me sad for her, not angry, because I knew my children were safe.

When my sister returned from her holiday I went back to my own house and my own family, and the following day my mother was rushed into hospital after suffering another stroke. I sat by her bed but I knew this time she would never recover. I thought of the last few weeks we'd shared, of her sitting in the bath while I gently wiped her skin with soapy bubbles. She'd sat there, smiling and remembering Somalian folk songs.

'Do you remember, Hibo?' she'd asked. And when I said I did, she'd begged me to sing for her.

'But I have a horrible voice, Hoyo,' I'd tried.

'It doesn't matter, just sing,' she'd said.

So as I dipped the cloth into the warmth of the bath, and made her skin shine with the water, I sang to her and she'd joined in, and every so often I pulled her near and planted a kiss on the side of her head. Just like she'd done to me that morning. She died a week after the second stroke, and I was devastated.

Now she was gone, and her old beliefs died with her. I remain convinced that had Hoyo lived for another ten years and seen how my life was to change, and how my role as an activist would gather strength, I could have convinced her that FGM is abuse and has no place in today's world. Two years after I lost Hoyo, my son Adam was born in 2006, followed by another daughter, Ikram, a year later. Yusuf and I doted on her just like we had all the others, and knew that she would be safe too. But deep down inside, it was becoming increasingly difficult for me to ignore what was going on in my own community, increasingly difficult to ignore my suspicion that girls were getting cut here in London. And yet I wasn't strong enough to move on from the past and face it fully. That would come though. It had to.

12

Halima's Tears

Every morning, the kitchen of our Walthamstow home would be filled with the noisy clatter of cutlery and china as my children chattered over breakfast. Instead of standing at the stove, ladling *anjero* batter into a hot pan as my mother once had, I filled our dining table with brightly coloured boxes of cereal that my British children gobbled up, leaving just the odd hoop, flake or splash of milk in the wake of their bowls.

Four years had passed since Ikram was born and after seven children, Yusuf and I were sure that our family was complete. The children were our lives. Abdinasir was now twenty, a reserved and serious boy, studying at university to be a doctor; Ali, eighteen, was the funny one with the big personality; Amal, fifteen, was just like I had been at that age, honest and feisty; Aisha, eleven, was the mother hen even then, caring and responsible, always helping out with the younger children; Abdilahi, nine, was cheeky and smart; Adam, even at six, was the pretty boy, obsessed with getting his hair just right; and, although she was only five years old, Yusuf and I were convinced Ikram would one day grow up to be a lawyer, with her argumentative yet caring nature.

Yusuf would go off to his job working nine to five, and I would busy myself – just as my mum always had – with housework and home-cooked meals. Every second of every day I ploughed into my family, making sure that the kids were up to date with their homework, sitting with them at the kitchen table after school and going through what they'd learned each day. When Abdinasir had first started school and was having trouble getting to grips with maths, I'd volunteered in his classroom to learn the way his teacher taught them, and with each child I did the same, knowing in my heart that education was the key to their future success. I was happy, and despite everything I'd said to my own mother – how the last thing I wanted to do was turn into her – part of me could understand why she'd been so content to be at home with the family too. Except I wanted more for my children than our life in Mogadishu had allowed her. It was only after I'd checked every single one of their books, and only when I was sure they'd completed and understood every task set by their teacher, that I would let them sink into the sofa, a tangle of arms and legs, engrossed in the Technicolor world of cartoons.

Not a day went by when I didn't impress on them just what opportunities they had open to them living in Britain. 'You can be whatever you want to be,' I told each of them. 'The only thing that will stop you is you.' I wanted them to be British through and through; I wanted them to embrace everything this country had to offer. I didn't want them to be shackled by the old cultural traditions I had endured, so while I was friends with Somalian women, I encouraged my children to make lots of different friends at school and I shielded them from my own community. I dreaded the day when they would hear about things such as FGM and I knew when it happened I would talk to them about it, no subject would be out of bounds like it had been for me. But I enjoyed the years that rolled by without one of them asking me what it was; I savoured their ignorance and innocence in that respect, that they hadn't been forced to grow up as quickly as I had.

But after almost twenty years of bringing up children, of chatting with the other mums in the playground about *EastEnders* or *Coronation Street*, of really feeling like this country had embraced and accepted me, I realised I now wanted to fulfil my own ambition and become something more than just a mother. So when Ikram started in reception in 2011, I decided to volunteer at her school. One morning, as I dropped my four youngest children off, I asked the head teacher if there were any opportunities there for me to lend a hand. He looked at the deputy head for a moment before turning to me with a smile.

'I think we can do better than that, Hibo,' he said. He told me that the school had been given some funding to train parents who wanted to be teaching assistants. I would need to volunteer eighteen hours a week, and use my spare time to complete my studies and assignments. It sounded perfect. I started working at the school a few months later. I loved to see the children tearing round the playground, the girls so free and happy. Until one day I was sitting in the head teacher's office, with two Somalian parents I'd often said hello to in the playground. Their daughter was ten-year-old Halima, a girl I'd seen many times skipping with her friends at breaktime, or working hard in class. She was a slight girl, slender, and she always had a smile, except not today. My head teacher had asked me to sit in on the meeting; he hadn't given me any clue as to why, but it soon became apparent.

'We need to take her out of school to visit a sick relative in Somalia,' her father explained urgently.

I glanced at Halima, thick tears magnified her deep-brown eyes. She tried desperately to swallow them down each time one of her parents glanced her way, but her distress was plain to see. And I knew why. I knew what she feared, and suddenly the meeting room felt smaller and hotter as the realisation dawned on me fully.

The head teacher tried again.

'But Halima is just about to sit her SATs, she has been studying for them for a long time.'

Her mother and father shook their heads.

'Is there no one she could stay with while you go? A friend? A relative?'

'She must come with us,' her father insisted.

Halima looked up at me then with big pleading eyes; if I could have picked her up and run with her from that room, I would have done.

I didn't speak as my head teacher tried everything to convince them not to go, or to persuade them to leave Halima in the UK, but they were adamant. The decision had already been made.

'We will only be away for two weeks,' Halima's father said. 'She won't miss too much school.'

So it was agreed that if they could produce the airline tickets showing that the return journey was already booked, the school would grant them permission to go. But as I watched them lead her by the hand out of the office, I didn't see Halima, I saw a six-year-old me, and a chance to prevent the past being repeated, so I ran after them. I stopped her mother.

'Please listen to what the staff are saying,' I pleaded. 'Halima has been working so hard for her SATs, her education is so important.'

Her mother looked down. 'I know, but she needs to come to Somalia,' she said. And they left.

That moment, standing alone in the school corridor, was a real wake-up call for me. I had spent years in the Somalian community in London; I'd heard whispers about *gudnin*, but perhaps I'd closed my eyes and ears to the reality. Perhaps because Yusuf and I had decided not to cut our girls, I told myself others weren't doing it either. After all, it was never spoken about openly, so it made it easier to pretend it wasn't happening. But not in that stuffy office – FGM had walked right up to me and tapped me on the shoulder. If our suspicions were right, it was happening here, not out there, not beyond Walthamstow, but right here, in our own school, and that thought made me feel physically sick. I was a part of that community and that culture, and yet I didn't truly know it was

131

happening, or at least I chose not to know, and so I was amazed that my employer had the same hunch. How did he even know about it? I had to ask him.

'What do you think is going on?' I had to hear him say it.

'We have real fears that she may be subjected to female genital mutilation.'

He told me Halima had been crying to her teacher, saying that she didn't want to go to Somalia, but she wouldn't say why, which had aroused their suspicions.

'You *know* about FGM?' I asked him, wide-eyed with surprise because I'd read nothing about it in the school's child protection policy. It was the first time I'd heard it spoken to me, or even said it myself out loud outside of our home, and I was amazed that the head teacher of a British school would even know what it was.

'Of course I've heard about FGM,' he said. 'But it's so difficult to prove.' That's why he'd asked me to sit in on the meeting, in case I knew for sure what was going on. But, just like him, I couldn't say with every certainty, only instinct. And my instinct told me he might just be right.

That evening, back at home, I couldn't stop thinking of Halima. Each time I closed my eyes I pictured her little face, and her tears.

'You tried your best,' Yusuf said, saying what he could to console me. 'But you can't stop her parents doing this; we can only look after our own girls.'

'But why would they do it?' I sobbed. 'Why would a mother do that to her child knowing the pain it causes?'

Images of Halima at home flooded my mind; did she overhear

her parents discussing it? I thought it unlikely, knowing full well that our community would never talk about it openly. But she knew enough to make her sob to her teachers and was brave enough to try to get them to help. And that, all of a sudden, made me feel incredibly angry. The thought of her being helpless to stop what was happening; perhaps being persuaded by her family that she must submit to this rite of passage in order to become a woman; being told, like so many girls before her, that she had to be brave.

I thought of how innocent I'd been before my cutting – just like Halima – and precisely what I had been robbed of afterwards. And I decided then that I had a voice, I could speak up for her. But how? Because I knew it wasn't just Halima; when I really thought about it, over the last year I'd been a teaching assistant there must have been other girls who were going through the same fears, who weren't as brave as Halima to speak out, who didn't even know if they would be heard. And if I really forced myself to think, there were also girls in my own community, in my own social circle; they hadn't come and confronted me like Halima's story had, but I could think of plenty who had been taken out of the country and who had returned smaller, quieter versions of their young exuberant selves.

I mentally scanned through memories I'd deliberately buried and I hated myself now for not being strong enough to speak out, to report those mothers to the police. Just like so many, I had turned my face away from abuse. I hadn't asked the questions because I was too scared of the answers. I'd remained content in the knowledge that my own children were safe, but now, I asked myself, what about all the others? Seeing it that day, right there in front of me, a young girl sobbing over her fate which was already sealed, I knew then that I couldn't hide from it any longer.

As I began setting the table for our evening meal, seething with rage and frustration, I remembered that part of my teaching-assistant coursework required us to write an essay on an abuse we felt strongly about. We'd discussed many different forms of child abuse in class and the warning signs to look out for, but no one had written about FGM. I knew my head teacher was aware of it, but he wasn't sure how to tackle it. I spooned the dinner on to the plates, and as the steam swirled up into the air, my plan came together in my head. The kids sat down to eat, and as they did, I turned quietly to Yusuf and said, 'I'm going to write about what happened to me.'

He put down the knife and fork he'd been about to use to tuck into his lamb *odka*, rice and spinach.

'Are you sure?' he said. 'Do you think you're ready?'

I nodded yes.

'I need to do it for girls like Halima, I need to tell people exactly what FGM is, that it's more than just three letters, about what it does to a girl, what it takes away from her, I need to help try and stop it.'

Yusuf took a deep breath.

'Do you really think you can change people's minds?' he asked.

'I have to try,' I told him.

So after we'd got the kids to bed, I sat with my laptop in the living room while Yusuf sat on the stairs – I'd told him I wanted to be totally alone to write; I knew it was going to be hard and I didn't want him to see me break down. But he refused to go to bed; instead, he stayed out of the room but close enough in case I needed him. It was hard going back to that day and, with each word I typed, the little details came back to me ever stronger: the cutter's cold, impassive face, her terrible tools, the smell of blood in the heat. Each time I felt myself crack and crumble under the weight of my own story, Yusuf was beside me, an arm around my shoulder, a tissue to wipe away my tears.

'You don't need to do this now,' he told me.

'I do,' I said. 'It's important.'

I just closed my eyes and thought of Halima, and the image of her desolation was enough to keep me writing, however painful it was. More memories flooded in of the barbaric and medieval abuse I'd suffered – the sense of abandonment, the hours that passed in a haze of burning, the stench of urine, the agonisingly slow process of weeing. It was as if by opening that small gap in my mind, the ugliness of all those years ago seeped in like an acrid smoke, blackening everything in the world I lived in now, leaving its sooty fingerprints on all that was good and clean and new. I'd convinced myself that being in Britain was enough for me to leave the past behind, but on dark nights when I couldn't sleep or at dawn when I'd woken up too early even for the birds, I'd imagined the girls back in Somalia. But in my mind they'd been thousands of miles away, they weren't in London, at my Walthamstow school. They weren't running around the playground with my own children.

And so I kept writing, and by the time I'd finished it was almost time to get the children up for school. I applied my black eyeliner thick that morning, as if it might somehow hide the lack of sleep and my puffy eyes. But I was armed with more than just make-up. At school I printed off four copies of my own story of FGM: one for the head teacher, and one each for my eldest children, the two boys – Abdinasir, by now twenty-two, and Ali, twenty – and my eldest girl, Amal, seventeen. It wasn't just time to tell my employers my story – it was time to tell my own family.

After the head had seen all the pupils arrive safely at school, I followed him to his office. There, I went in and shut the door behind me.

'I need you to read this,' I said, placing the printout in front of him. 'It's important.'

It was only a six-page document, yet I felt as if the weight of it had landed on his desk with a heavy thud. He picked it up and started to read, and as I stood in front of his desk and I watched his eyes scan the paper from left to right, he was soon overcome with emotion.

When he finished it, he looked up at me, clearly moved.

'Hibo, I had no idea this happened to you,' he said quietly, as he put my assignment down. 'But I promise you that from now on FGM will be in our child protection policy.'

Already, with this one small act, I had made a difference. He got up and left the office and when he returned he had two deputy heads with him. I sat with them as they both read the same transcript.

'You need to share this with the rest of the staff,' one of them said, running her hand over her face.

But I shook my head, overwhelmed by the prospect. That was 120 people.

'No,' I insisted. 'This was only for you,' I said, looking to the head teacher.

I was known among my colleagues as Hibo the joker, as someone who was fun, who always wore a wide smile. I didn't want them to think of me as a freak. All my very worst fears about how FGM had, in my mind, singled me out rushed up from my belly, lying heavy on my chest. I didn't want my friends to look at me differently, and yet I knew that this was a story they also needed to read if we were going to protect more children. So I agreed to think about it.

That night, I left school with the remaining copies destined for three readers who meant more to me than anyone. My two eldest sons were out so I placed a copy on each of their beds, and then I handed one to Amal. She glanced up at me quizzically when she saw the title and the name of the author.

'What's this, Mum?' she asked.

'I'd like you to read it.'

I sat across the living room from her as the story that had taken me all night, a thousand tears – and a lifetime – to write was eaten up by Amal's eyes in a matter of minutes. When she looked up at me, I saw that they were glistening with tears.

'Why didn't you tell me about this before?' she said. 'I had no idea this had happened to you.'

I nodded.

'But I thought we talked about everything,' she said. 'How could you not tell me about this when it was such a huge thing that happened to you?'

I could see she was upset for me, but there was something else in her eyes too, an anger perhaps that I hadn't told her about it before, that I thought she couldn't handle the truth. Maybe even betrayal. I needed to explain.

'This was a conversation I needed to have myself first,' I told her. 'I'm sorry I never discussed this with you, but I haven't been able to speak to anyone about it apart from your father until now.'

She turned the essay over in her hands, as if examining its contents while the full meaning of it sank in, a secret about her mother she never knew.

'You kept the biggest part of your life a secret from me,' she said.

I'd always vowed to be open with my children, but now I realised that she was looking at me in the same way I had looked at my mother, and all I could say was sorry.

'It consumed me for so many years,' I said. 'But now I'm in a position to tell you.'

I think, just like all children, she appreciated my honesty.

'I have heard of FGM,' she said. 'I had a friend at school and she was cut.'

Now she was telling me something I didn't know. For years I'd thought I'd been shielding her from a truth, but she knew about it all the time.

'Why didn't you ask me about it?' I asked her.

'I didn't know how,' she replied.

When she was younger, I remember asking her if she had any

Somalian friends at school and what they talked about, trying to find out whether FGM was something she might have heard of from them. But it seemed to me that she didn't know a thing about it and, back then, that's how I wanted it to stay. Now, though, it was time for *me* to tell her.

'I did hear about it, but it never seemed important because I just knew it was something you wouldn't do to us,' Amal said.

And that in itself was success.

'I can't believe this happened to you,' she said, spotting my tears and crossing the room to wrap me in a hug. 'You are so courageous, and such a wonderful mum. Thank you so much for protecting me.'

We talked a little more that evening in the way that only mothers and daughters can – or should be able to. When my boys got home they read it too, but they didn't want to ask me questions like Amal had.

'I only heard about FGM recently as part of my medical training,' Abdinasir said. 'But I never thought it would have happened to you, Mum.'

And all three of my children agreed on one thing – that they were proud of me for finally telling my story. Their reaction, along with that of the head teacher and his deputies, convinced me that I needed to share my story wider still. A week later, I stood in an empty school assembly hall. It was the end of another day, and slowly the hum of children chattering as their parents collected them from school was replaced with silence in the playground as the last ones left through the gates.

In one hand, I clutched my essay, those three letters – FGM – now as familiar to me as my own name. Slowly, my colleagues started filtering in and taking up the rows of seats that had been laid out by the caretaker. The empty hall was filled with the quiet conversations of the staff, tired from a day's teaching, but curious to know why I was standing in front of them. Finally, the head introduced me. I was by now forty-two – it had taken me thirty-six years to speak about what had happened to me back in Mogadishu, and within days I'd gone from telling my children to addressing a hall packed with people. But as I stepped up to the microphone at the front of the room, on legs that I felt sure were about to give way, I knew that it was time for somebody to speak out, and if not me, then who?

I cleared my throat. 'Hello everyone,' I said tremulously, and I heard my voice waver.

So many faces stared in my direction, some I had come to think of as friends, others were my bosses and mentors, but none of them knew the secret that I hid deep inside. I closed my eyes and thought of Halima. And that's who I spoke up for.

'I want to tell you my story,' I started. 'You might find it uncomfortable, but it's one that you should know.'

I started off by telling them about the four different types of FGM, and how it was Type 3 that was carried out on me. I did feel exposed; it was incredibly hard for me to divulge to them that under the colourful dresses I wore to school, under my *abaya*, I had been mutilated. That as I'd joked with them in the canteen, or stood at the school gates looking like any other British mum, something separated me from them. I was different. I had been abused as a child and, tearfully, I told them what had been done, how it had been done and by whom.

When I'd finished, I looked out at a sea of faces, many of them wet with their own tears, and for a few minutes, as I gathered my breath, nothing filled the school hall except a heavy silence as the weight of what I'd told them sank in. Finally, someone spoke, and once they did, it was like the floodgates opening.

'I remember one girl a few years ago, she went to Somalia and when she returned she was never the same ...'

'I had a pupil a few years ago who suddenly became very withdrawn ...'

'I mentioned my fears to a former head teacher of mine but she said that it was their culture and we shouldn't interfere ...'

I felt the loneliness of every child that my colleagues mentioned they'd come across over the years. Many of the girls they talked about were in Year Two or Three, the same age as my Ikram, and that thought alone was enough to turn my stomach inside out with horror. Now they'd heard my story, more and more stories of their own began to surface, and so did more and more questions.

'Is it a religious practice?' someone asked.

'No!' I said. 'There is nothing in the Koran that says girls should be cut. It is purely a cultural practice and it is one hundred per cent child abuse.'

The weight of that statement settled in the room, and I knew it changed everything. Perhaps people had tiptoed around the subject thinking that they needed to respect a religious belief, but now that they knew the plain truth, I could see their understanding of it grow in a second. This was not a religious command, it was a choice, and just as Yusuf and I had made the choice not to have our daughters cut, so too could every other mother and father.

'Religion should never be used as an excuse for abusing a child,' I told the staff, and they nodded. I felt liberated and empowered. And I realised that by talking about it, I stood a chance of saving one more girl.

Finally, the talk was over, and as I left the stage, staff came up to me one by one to congratulate me.

'You were so brave to speak out,' one said.

'I had no idea,' another said.

My colleagues were incredible and so supportive; they had made me feel safe to tell my story. Many of them came to hug me, some were in tears, others angry that this could happen to little girls, but all of them were determined that this message needed to be heard.

'You have to talk to staff at other schools,' my head teacher said.

The other teaching staff nodded.

'They need to hear about this too, Hibo,' someone else said. 'It's so important.'

I decided there and then that I would use my own trauma to educate others. I'd spent my whole life feeling sad that FGM had shaped so much of my story, but in that moment, as the staff filtered from the room, energised, determined and grateful to me for my honesty, I realised it could be a blessing too, because my own experiences might just change another girl's future.

13

Spreading the Word

It had been barely three months since I had first addressed the teaching staff at Mission Grove School, but here I was, on stage again, staring out at rows of attentive faces. The council chamber I was about to speak to was only meant to hold 100, and yet it was alive with the expectant hum of nearly 300 people. I had already given another talk to teaching staff at a school in Leyton, and I felt now the growing wave of action picking up more and more momentum as my story rolled off the platform. These were all people who were rallying themselves in the fight against FGM; who sat up in their chairs that little bit higher when they realised that FGM wasn't just something I knew about, but something I had gone through myself. And the shame that I'd felt at being potentially labelled a freak had long since been erased by the numerous emails praising me for being brave enough to speak out. But what pleased me most was that people were willing to listen.

My friend and school counsellor, Claire Colgill, had arranged the talk today, and the pair of us sat on the stage as she began to interview me about my own story. I answered her questions with absolute honesty, not missing out one bit of my account. I saw people shift uncomfortably in their seats, I saw them cross and uncross their legs, and often I saw their tears, too, as they imagined themselves in the place of a six-year-old girl who had been pinned down while her own flesh was sliced off in front of her bulging eyes. I wanted them to hear those details, every single one of them, no matter how hard it was, because I wanted my words to leave my mouth and fly across the council chamber, pricking at their consciences in the hope that they might in turn protect another girl. The council chamber that night was packed not just with teachers, but with people from the education department, social workers, police officers and members of the general public as well.

Four months had passed now since we'd sat in my head teacher's office with Halima's parents, and she hadn't been returned to school as they'd promised. The return air tickets that they produced later turned out to be fakes. They also took their eldest daughter from secondary school without the school's consent. Neither of those girls ever returned. The best I could hope for was that their parents, fearing an intervention from the school or social services, had moved away. The worst fear was that their slight bodies had succumbed to shock or infection in a hut not unlike the one in which I had lain. But at night, when I flopped into bed

144

beside Yusuf, exhausted from a day at school and then another talk at a council chamber or school, I only had to think of them in order to feel reinvigorated about the fight. I wondered why the pull of this cultural tradition was still so strong for some parents, when I'd been able to turn my back on it so easily. Draining as it was, speaking to a room of people about my personal experience seemed a small sacrifice to make compared to the danger these girls faced, and, in a way, vocalising what had been done to me was my own form of therapy.

Soon, the local newspaper was contacting me, asking me to write a piece about my own FGM and the work I was doing with schools to educate teachers about the signs to look out for. My head teacher had told other local principals that I had an important message which they needed to hear; so, often at the end of the school day, I'd hurry to the other side of Walthamstow, sometimes with my children in tow, to speak in front of another assembly hall full of teachers. 'Thank you for listening this afternoon,' I'd tell them, so much more confidently than the first time I'd had to talk into a microphone. And then professionals further afield heard about my work in Walthamstow. The Metropolitan Police contacted me at the school to ask if I'd give a talk to some of their officers.

'I don't know if I can do it,' I said to Yusuf. 'What will I talk to the police about?'

'You can,' he said. 'You'll think of something.'

I met with an officer from the Metropolitan Police, just one at first, and I gave her the same talk as I had everyone about the basics of FGM and what was done to me. And then I moved on to the law.

'I realise this practice has been illegal since 1985 in this country,' I said. 'But the key to stopping FGM isn't just prosecutions.'

She sat up in her chair and listened.

'What you have to remember is that the mother who has it done to her daughter is a victim too, even if she doesn't know it. She was also abused as a child in the same way and she doesn't realise it's bad; she only thinks she's doing the right thing for her daughter – not to cause her pain – but to better secure her future. The police fight against FGM has to be more about prevention than anything else, because even the ones who carry it out are victims themselves, and the best thing you can do is help them to see this.'

Next came the medical professionals: midwives wanted me to speak to them about FGM, and this meant so much to me. I remember the first day I arrived at King's College Hospital in London to give a talk. The smell of the sterile corridors, the doors to the wards kept firmly shut, and staff shuffling between them, all reminded me of the birth of each of my children, and especially of Abdinasir's delivery, when I arrived in hospital knowing hardly any English and went through such an intimate experience without anyone explaining to me why I looked different, or even acknowledging that I did, instead just writing it in my notes – it was as if I wasn't even there. After I explained the basics to the group of midwives who had come to hear my talk, I told them about my own births, about what would have helped me.

'You are clinical professionals,' I told them. 'But you need to remember that you're also human and you're dealing with other

146

human beings. You need to talk to the women as you would a friend, ask them what happened to them – don't ignore it.'

I think this was one of the first times that these midwives had been encouraged to communicate about FGM; it was as though I'd given them permission to talk to their patients, assuring them that a lot of these women would actually be *pleased* if they had someone to talk to. In those early days that was one of the most empowering talks I gave, knowing how much I'd suffered giving birth to my own children; it was an incredible feeling to think that I might make a difference to even just a few women who were about to go through pregnancy and birth having undergone FGM.

Each sector I engaged with would have their own important contribution to make, from the teachers who could look out for the warning signs at school, to the police who would realise that mothers are victims too, to the midwives who would see these women through one of the most personal moments of their lives and hold on to their hands a little tighter knowing what they'd been through. These developments and changes in attitude all stemmed from one thing: education. And as more and more secondary schools in the area started contacting me to ask if I would speak to their teachers, my determination to spread the message grew stronger.

But the reaction wasn't all positive.

I'd met my friend Maryam when I'd moved into our first flat in London. She was Somalian too, around my age, and we both had young children. We'd take the kids to the park together, celebrate Eid together; we went to the cinema, and we chatted about almost everything. I knew she was cut, not because we spoke about it openly but because, when her husband left her, she wondered if it was because she couldn't give him a satisfactory sex life.

'It's because of what was done to me as a child,' Maryam said, cursing her parents for putting her through it, convinced that this was why her husband had been living as man and wife with another woman for a number of years. I could see how upset she was. 'I'm here for you, whatever you decide to do,' I told her, unsure as to whether she might consider taking him back at some point.

But when news of my activism spread, it seemed I couldn't expect the same loyalty from her. I hadn't told Maryam what I was doing at first, not even the little things like speaking at my school, but then I didn't tell anyone. Perhaps, somewhere deep down inside, I knew that she would disapprove; perhaps I didn't want her or anyone else pouring scorn on something that made me feel so alive, so engaged. Perhaps I wasn't ready to be challenged about my decision to speak out, so I'd just kept it to myself, following my own heart. The biggest thing for me was that Yusuf was on my side, nobody else mattered.

My confidence grew as I saw the reaction of people inside the education system, and realised the level of support there was for me out there, so one day, as Maryam and I sat having coffee and biscuits in my house, I cleared my throat and decided it was now or never. Maryam and I shared everything together – we were similar, strong, outspoken women – so I took a deep breath and before I knew it the words had left my mouth.

'I've been talking at my school about FGM,' I said. 'Telling the teaching staff exactly what it is and why it is done.'

148

Maryam stopped, her hot cup of coffee hovering somewhere between the table and her mouth. Her jaw hung open, her eyes wide, and I swallowed down my coffee, feeling it burn the back of my throat.

'What?' she said.

'I'm telling them about *gudnin*, what they did to us.'

She put down her coffee cup.

'But people will be against you,' she said. 'They won't like what you've done.'

I looked at her then, my friend, and in that instant I felt betrayed. How could she immediately think of what others thought instead of how important this was?

'I don't care what people think of me. Teachers need to know the truth, pupils need to know. We need to stop this.'

Maryam was brushing down her skirt as if suddenly she was ready to get up and leave.

'We should talk about this, Maryam,' I said.

But she was muttering about all the things she needed to get on with at home and rounding up the children.

After I shut the door behind her, I felt disappointment reverberating in my chest.

'What did you expect?' Yusuf said when he came home and I told him about Maryam's reaction. 'Not everyone is going to feel the same as you, Hibo.' But I expected that Maryam would. Or at the very least that she would have listened to and supported me. I didn't see her for a few days after that. I invited her over, eager to talk, but she made excuses that she was busy. Then the weeks passed and even the replies to my text messages started to dwindle. We always used to go along to weddings together, but now if Maryam was invited, I would only know about it if I spotted her heading out, all dressed up in a colourful *hijab*. I got the message, but it still stung. I stopped trying to invite her for coffee; I told the children she was busy when they wanted to play with her kids.

Meanwhile, news of my activism was making its way around Walthamstow. National newspapers wanted to write about my talks; it was surreal to sit at the breakfast table with my children as they hungrily spooned cereal into their mouths while my face stared up at us all from the *Guardian* or the *Telegraph*.

'You're famous, Mum,' Ikram grinned up at me. I could see I was making them proud and so I had to push thoughts of Maryam from my mind. My activism started to take on a life of its own and I was proud of myself too.

Many weeks now went by without Maryam and me setting eyes on each other, and, living as close as we did, that was no easy feat. But when I heard her daughter Naima was in hospital with pneumonia, I wanted to be there for my friend when she needed me most. Yusuf and I took our youngest two children to the hospital to see her, but the welcome wasn't a warm one.

Maryam looked me up and down from her daughter's bedside.

'I was at a wedding the other day,' she said. 'Everyone was talking about you.'

I glanced down at Adam and Ikram, but she continued regardless.

'They were cursing and saying things about you. They asked

me, "Do you know this woman?" And I told them, "I've never met her in my life."'

She laughed then, but her words had cut right through me, so I bent down and kissed Naima. 'I hope you feel better soon, darling,' I said, then hurried my two children from the room.

In the car, I burst into tears. I wished so much that I'd been able to tell her how disappointed I was, how hurt I was, but I wouldn't have spoken like that to her in front of Naima. Not that it stopped her in front of my children.

'That wasn't a very nice thing to say,' Ikram's tiny voice said from the back of the car.

'Just forget about it,' I told her, as Yusuf put the car into gear and we snaked out of the hospital grounds.

I decided that day that I didn't want anything more to do with Maryam. This was a woman I'd grown to know and love, I'd confided in, a woman with whom I'd shared the births of my children, and yet when I needed her most she'd looked the other way. What was most unbelievable to me was that even though she was thousands of miles away from Somalia, away from the life we'd grown up in, she still protected a cultural practice that I knew had taken its toll on her, just like it had done on me. She'd lost a husband, her children had lost their father, and yet she wouldn't stand up and say that FGM was brutal and that it shouldn't be carried out on little girls. Instead, she was more concerned about what other people thought of me – and, as a consequence, of her. She was part of this community that was determined to keep FGM shrouded in secrecy. She was no friend. We shared much less than I'd ever realised.

151

CUT

This was a situation I was forced to get used to and I developed a thick skin. I stopped going to the weddings of people in the Somalian community where I lived, knowing that I would meet with a frosty reception, that my hands wouldn't be welcome to dip into the plates full of *odka* or *halwa*. I would instead be handed cynicism and criticism. Most Somalian people valued their traditions and they saw me as a threat to that. And yet it was frustrating because they were the very people I needed to get through to.

There was one wedding I ventured to attend a few months later. If I'd wanted to avoid drawing attention to myself, though, I went about it the wrong way. I arrived late and, when I walked in, everybody turned around thinking it was the bride making her entrance. I shuffled to my seat, embarrassed, and after the ceremony a woman I'd never met before came over to me.

'Why do you talk about us?' she said. 'Why do you tarnish our culture?'

I looked away from her at first, wanting to disappear. But then I remembered my cause and I sat up straighter. I turned my face to her then, looking her square in the eyes.

'Us?' I asked. 'I specifically remember talking about *my* vagina. Just mine. And using *my* name, not yours.'

Her eyes widened in shock. She sucked in air and puffed out her chest as people sitting around me sniggered into their napkins.

'You are even crazier than I thought,' she said, standing up and bustling away, weaving her exit between the tables.

The others at my table applauded.

'Well done,' they said.

But for every ten people who supported me, it was hard to ignore that one who didn't, especially when they came from within my own family. I never spoke to my sister Hadsan about my work; instinct told me that we would never agree. I knew that she knew what I was doing, though, and my niece had told me that she kept cuttings of the newspaper articles that featured me, but she only ever acknowledged my talks once.

'Hibo, why are you doing this?' she asked as we made food together one weekend.

I stopped and turned to her, knowing exactly what she was referring to. 'Do you really want to get into this?'

She paused for a moment and then looked away, continuing to chop vegetables into fine crescents. Here was another woman I'd grown up with, emancipated by our move to a different country, yet still determined to hold on to old cultural traditions. None of these people, or their reactions, would put me off. Not now that I had started. I'd had a taste of the difference I might be able to make and I knew I could do more.

Two months later, I was at a meeting chaired by our local Labour MP, Stella Creasy. I'd felt intimidated by all the women there; some ran schools and councils and others had been active campaigners for far longer than me. But I met a woman called Jenny who, after hearing my story, invited me to talk at her secondary school. It was my dream to speak to schoolchildren directly because educating them about FGM would give them a better chance of protecting themselves. I wanted to empower girls, so that they would not be pressured by their parents; I wanted to educate boys, so that they would tell their own parents that they didn't want a girl who'd been cut; and I wanted to inform those outside of the community, so that they would be able to help and protect their friends at risk.

Just weeks later, as I walked into the grounds of Jenny's school, I was shaking with nerves. Its tall frontage seemed so imposing, packed with three storeys of children. How on earth was I going to say what I needed to say? I felt on my shoulders, under the bright-purple *hijab* I was wearing, the heavy responsibility of the talk I was about to give them as I crossed the school's forecourt and headed towards reception. I didn't know how many of the children would even have heard of FGM. I didn't know whether I'd be talking to pupils who had been victims themselves, or if they were at risk of becoming victims. I had no idea how they might feel if I described FGM as child abuse. But I knew that, as a teenager, I'd longed for someone to speak openly to me about what I'd been through. When you are a child who has suffered abuse you don't see beauty in the world, you don't see the flowers and trees and animals and people anymore, just your own loneliness. There isn't a world that is tangible outside of your own hurt and pain. You look only inwards as your mind is swallowed up with a million whys that will never be answered unless someone offers you what I was about to offer these students. There could be girls inside this building who were going through that right now.

As a child I'd wanted honesty from the adults around me and the chance to have my voice heard. That's exactly what I needed to give these children. I didn't have to sugar-coat anything for them,

I just needed to tell them the facts, and they didn't even have to agree with me; what they decided to do with the information after I left was up to them. But, I reminded myself, knowledge is power, and I was being given the opportunity to empower 180 Year Nine students. Could I have imagined having that chance six months ago? Never. Things had changed so quickly and now here I was, on a mission to enlighten.

Half an hour later, Jenny was introducing me to the packed assembly hall. The students looked up at me from the floor with varying shades of curiosity painted across their faces. There was silence as Jenny began to speak.

'I'm going to introduce you to this lady and in my book she is the most brave and honest person I have ever met,' she said.

Every gaze was on me.

'Today she is going to talk to you about something very dear to her heart which affects you and affects other children just like you. You need to listen very carefully.'

My heart was racing in my chest, the fullness of the responsibility pounding against my ribcage.

The room bristled with anticipation as I took Jenny's place on the stage.

'Hello, I'm Hibo,' I said. My greeting was met by silence, broken only by a handful of muffled hellos.

I tried again, this time louder. 'I can't hear you!' I cried across the hall. 'Hello!'

And the school hall rang with their chorus. I had their attention now. I'd broken the tension between us and now we could all relax.

'How many of you have heard of FGM?' I asked the hall, watching as just a few hands made their way awkwardly into the air.

'Well, I'm here to tell you what it is.'

I started, just like with the adults, with the descriptions of the different types. I told them that it happened to children just like them, often to toddlers, sometimes babies, and how it was carried out. I watched them wriggle as I spoke; some looked down into their laps, most eyes never left me.

'But what is most important,' I said, 'what I really need you to know is that it is child abuse.'

During those forty minutes, I went through all the medical complications resulting from FGM, explained their human rights to them and told them what they needed to know to keep themselves safe. I drummed into them that should they feel in danger at home they should dial 999, or if they were abroad they should get a message to the British embassy and help would come. Then, finally, one young student put up her hand.

'Has this happened to you, miss?' her voice sounded small in the huge hall, but my reply was loud and confident.

'Yes,' I said.

A collective gasp went up in the hall, but rather than feeling small for confessing that I had been mutilated, rather than feeling like a freak like I'd done before, I left that stage feeling invigorated. Those children – boys and girls, black and white – connected with me on a very human level and it felt wonderful.

And from those very humble beginnings, my diary quickly filled with the scratches of different-coloured Biros as I added more and more talks in schools to my schedule. At each of them I'd look out and see the same recognition and empathy and sense of empowerment. I left behind at each school the excited chatter of children who were determined to stand up for their friends who might be at risk.

Of course, I never knew the stories behind the students I was addressing; I had no idea whether what I was saying would resonate with them, whether they'd go home and tell their parents, their community, whether it would save their lives. I could only hope, but as I packed away my slides after a talk at one local sixth-form college a few months later, I noticed that one student was lingering long after the others had left the hall. Her head was covered, like mine, but her eyes betrayed a real need to talk to me. I went over to her.

'Hello,' I said, and as I did, her eyes filled with tears. I took her hands. 'Come and sit down here with me.'

She did as I asked, and as I talked softly to her, asking her what was wrong, she broke down further.

'Your talk . . .' she said, between sobs. 'I knew what you were talking about . . . It's happened to me.'

She put her head into her lap as I rubbed her back.

'It's OK,' I said. 'You've been very brave to tell me.'

After a few moments, she looked up again.

'Everything you said about how long it takes to go for a wee, how painful your periods are, it's the same for me,' she said. But there was something else, something that she wasn't telling me. I sensed there was another reason she was reaching out to me.

157

'You can tell me anything,' I said, noticing her hands trembling in mine.

'My sisters . . .' she said, finally. 'They're younger than me and I think the same is going to happen to them.'

My eyes briefly flitted up to the college teacher who had arranged the talk, who had hovered close by ever since this girl had broken from the crowd of students to wait behind. What she'd just told me was a child-protection issue, and I was aware that after her hands left mine the relevant authorities would need to be involved, that she would have to give more details, that her parents would be contacted. But while her hands were in mine, all I could do was soothe her, and tell her over and over that she'd done the right thing.

'Your sisters need protection,' I told her. 'And by speaking out, you've made sure they'll get it.'

It took me weeks to get the image of her from my head. For days afterwards, each time I closed my eyes I could see her wide and worried eyes, I could feel her hands in mine.

'The college will be looking after her now,' Yusuf assured me. I had to accept there was nothing more I could do, confidentiality meant that I couldn't even get any information about her from the college.

It was a bittersweet victory for me in the early days of my campaigning, though, because these were precisely the girls I wanted to reach and yet, at the same time, it was painful to witness that they were there at all. As my campaign gathered pace, I would stand in the doorway of my living room as my children sat cross-legged on the floor watching my appearances on the BBC or Sky

TV, glued to the screen. Afterwards they would turn around and applaud me, and I would laugh and bow to them.

Everyone was so supportive. One of the most amazing moments was speaking at Oxford University to a room crammed with hundreds of FGM and child-protection workers, doctors, psychologists and academics from all over Europe. But nothing compared to the sense of connection I felt when I spoke to the children. They, after all, were the next generation, the ones who could really make a difference. Many times after talks the children would come up to me at the end of lessons, saying they wanted to do more; and I was amazed by the number of students who would simply come over and ask if they could give me a hug.

'You're so brave,' they'd tell me. And being able to talk to them in a way I'd never been able to speak to my own mother, or my peers, was my way of healing too. Just by telling my story made it feel less secretive; it made the wounds inside heal. It couldn't change the past but it created a new future. It made me feel empowered by what had happened to me, rather than a victim.

One of the ways I'd tried to communicate with younger kids was to sit with them afterwards as they created anti-FGM posters. No words were off limits, no images banned; they could draw and express themselves however they liked. Afterwards, they'd pin them up in the school corridors. They were now doing my work for me! Each school I visited I left children engaged and ready for action. I took photographs of each image they produced and, at home at night, I'd flick through them on my phone, my heart bursting with pride. Months rolled by, and then a year, and demand for

159

my talks was only growing. I started working with Project Azure, a unit of the Metropolitan Police set up to counter FGM in the city. It was exhausting work: I'd be up at 6am getting the kids ready for school or college, and then do a full day's work before taking the youngest children home and then heading out to give another talk.

'I don't think I can keep this up,' I'd tell Yusuf, utterly worn out. But we needed the money from my teaching-assistant job and I wasn't going to cut down on my talks when I was making such amazing progress.

However, there were still some who were opposed to my work, even within my own family. In the summer of 2014, one of Yusuf's elderly relatives came to stay from Canada. We looked after her, ferrying her to visit people and making delicious food at home, but my work meant I wasn't around that much and sometimes she had to come along in the car while Yusuf took me to talks in the evenings. One night, as Yusuf was driving her home, she asked him what I was doing, and he told her that I was speaking out against FGM. It was only when I got home that night that Yusuf told me about her reaction.

'She couldn't believe I was letting you campaign against FGM,' he said. 'She was furious. She said I wasn't the man of the house, that I was under the thumb.'

I laughed then. 'Let her think what she likes,' I said, and we went to bed.

But in the early hours the phone calls from Somalia started.

I leant over, still sleepy, to grab the phone. It was Yusuf's family calling.

'It's for you,' I said, passing him the phone.

I heard the muffled sounds coming through the receiver, the shouting, the rambling as Yusuf tried to reply. But he couldn't get a word in. When he hung up, I asked him what it was about.

'They're saying that our girls should have been cut,' he said. Obviously, the old woman had called them and told them about my campaign, and putting two and two together they'd realised we'd never got our daughters cut. I had waited twenty years for this, and all I could think of was that conversation I'd had with Yusuf all those years before, that he had to stand up to his family just like I had mine.

I sighed. 'We had this conversation before you got into my pants,' I said.

'Don't put it that way!' Yusuf said, but he knew exactly what I was talking about.

'Now it's your time for action,' I reminded him.

I wasn't tense, I wasn't worried. I was adamant, and Yusuf knew that. He'd promised me all those years ago he'd deal with his family, and now he had to do just that.

The phone hadn't been back in its cradle for five minutes when it rang again.

'It's four in the morning!' I wailed to Yusuf. 'Tell them to stop.' And in the end I did it for him, by pulling the phone out of the socket.

I don't know what he said to them, I didn't want to know. But a couple of days later the phone calls ceased, and my work continued.

Then, in March 2015, I received a letter from my local council to

161

say that I had been nominated for their annual Love Your Borough awards, and the winner would be announced at a gala dinner at the town hall. I had to wipe away tears as I read the letter – to be recognised and nominated for an award was such a huge compliment. I took Abdilahi and Aisha along with me on the night, carefully applying the kohl under my eyes and dressing in a deep-blue *abaya* and a black headscarf trimmed with delicate silver thread. Not that I thought I would win. We sat through the ceremony, watching each winner go up to collect their award. And then, finally, it was time for them to announce the Leader's Individual Award. I sat patiently as they started to talk about the winner's story, a woman who had survived against the odds and now used her experience to educate others. It didn't sink in, not at first, and then Aisha turned to me across the table.

'They're talking about you, Mum!'

'... And the winner is Hibo Wardere!' the council chief announced.

Suddenly the room burst into applause and I was up on my feet, being directed to the stage. Abdilahi and Aisha were hugging me and clapping, brilliant smiles lighting up their faces. I was speechless. For once in my life I didn't know what to say because the sheer emotion spilling from my heart stole my voice from me, and all I could do was let tears run down my cheeks. As the audience rose to their feet to applaud my work, I realised that no other award would ever come close to the one that was presented to me in my local community. I held it up in my arms and left the stage, feeling so proud of myself and how far I had come.

And my luck wasn't over. Just a few weeks later, I got a call from the community-safety officer at the council. They were making funding available to tackle all aspects of FGM in the borough, from protecting children to treating survivors, and they'd created a special educational role: FGM Mediator for Waltham Forest Borough.

'I'd like you to apply,' he said.

I'd never wanted anything so much in all my life.

I was nervous. As I waited outside the meeting room, I wiped my clammy hands over and over on my *abaya*, yet they were instantly sticky again. Then the door opened and I was shown in. Behind the desk sat a panel of three people who grilled me for more than an hour. I knew I was the perfect person for the job, I had to be, and yet they didn't make it easy for me. The interview was tough, but I did what I always had – I told my story and talked about the passion I felt for the campaign.

A few days later, the post arrived at home, one letter marked with the borough council logo.

'This is it,' I told Yusuf.

I ripped open the letter and then burst into tears.

'It's mine,' I sobbed, looking up at him. 'The job is mine.'

I left Mission Grove School for the last time on a light summer's eve at the end of the school term and, as the gates closed behind me, hot tears welled in my eyes. I knew I was doing the right thing but it was still a wrench to leave. If it wasn't for the support I'd received there, if it wasn't for that first assignment, none of this would have been possible.

But as I sat down at my desk, in my new office, in my new role as an FGM mediator, it became harder to picture the little girl who had lain in that hut all alone, tears streaking her face, burning with just one question: why? Because not only had I answered it for myself, I was now able to answer it for so many others. The result of that is here in these pages; this is how far my journey has brought me. That first day I thought back to the conversations I'd had as a six-year-old at my mother's skirt – how I'd quizzed her about why she was so content to be at home cooking and cleaning, why she didn't want to go out and get a job and change the world – and it occurred to me that I'd achieved my goal: I had indeed become more than my mother.

14

Educating Men and Women in FGM-Practising Communities

*A*s I've watched my three daughters growing up, I've seen how they've fretted and worried about a great many things. At six years old, they were worrying about who was going to play with them at school, or about whether their best friend would be able to sit next to them in class, or about why their friend was playing with someone else at playtime. My youngest daughter, Ikram, now worries about what toy she'll get for her ninth birthday. My fifteen-year-old, Aisha, worries about whether she'll pass the GCSE exams she's got coming up at school. And my eldest daughter, Amal, who is nineteen, worries about her university studies. Although every life decision might be a cause of concern for my girls, each milestone is a delight for me to witness, because it is so far removed from my own anxiety, and that of my peers, at that age. It is a world and a generation apart. The only thing we talked about in the playground at six was who had been cut and who needed to be cut.

To bring the brutal tradition of FGM to an end, education must begin first and foremost within the practising communities. In Somalia, we were brought up by women, we were fed by women, bathed by women, put to bed by women. It seems so contradictory to me that these women are the same people who perpetuate the myth that FGM is valuable to a girl. If they wield such influence over children, and girls in particular, if they know the pain that each and every one has to go through in order to be cut, how can they continue to facilitate such abuse? Given the very basic instincts of being a mother, of wanting to protect your child from pain or fear of death, how can you order the mutilation of your own daughter? How can you see her suffer like you yourself have suffered? Tradition to them appears to be far more important than blood ties. Maintaining custom and ritual among their people outweighs the horror of the suffering that they are prepared to see their daughters undergo. Being judged by their community seems far more important than the risk of losing their little girl.

The answers to these questions lie in the simple truth that these women have no idea that the mutilation that has occurred between their legs is abuse and that they themselves are victims. These are the women who will tell you that they were cut and it hasn't done them any harm; but that is because they don't know any different, not because they haven't lived with the same painful and uncomfortable side effects as other FGM survivors. They just haven't made the association between the constant infections and the cutting they received as a child. They think all women suffer like this; this is just what it is to be a woman.

To these women it is a rite of passage to be endured on the way to womanhood and it is also a security, a form of protection. The cutting will keep you clean; it will strip you of your natural desire; it will mean that your family is not judged; and, one day, it will hopefully ensure that your own child marries well, into a family just as upstanding as your own, thereby reinforcing the security of your family. To these mothers, FGM is not about needless pain, it is about survival. That is why my mother was cut, and her mother before her, and so on.

It is a tradition so entrenched in such communities, an act and a belief system passed down from generation to generation, that most women in these cultures don't even think to question it. Those mothers who do challenge the practice face ostracism and isolation – a 2013 UNICEF report acknowledged that women who don't repeat the same procedure on their own daughters may be liable to 'social exclusion, criticism, stigma, inability to find their daughter suitable marriage partners'.* In a small community, that is a lot to risk. Even in cases where there are laws to prevent FGM occurring, the report went on to state that the fear of social exclusion for not conforming to the norm may be stronger than the fear of fines or imprisonment. Legislation alone cannot make families give up a centuries-old tradition.

* 'Female Genital Mutilation/Cutting: A statistical overview and exploration of the dynamics of change', UNICEF, 2013.

According to the report, a massive 93 per cent of women and girls in Ghana wanted to see an end to FGM. That's the kind of figure you'd expect to see – in fact, it's the other 7 per cent that it is surely harder to fathom. And yet, as you go down the list of countries, support for the abolition wanes, with just 33 per cent of Somalian women and girls in favour of its eradication, and just 19 per cent of females in Guinea. I find these figures disappointing – without women themselves saying no to FGM, what hope do we have of saving children?

Agnes Pareyio co-founded the Tasaru Ntomonok Initiative, which runs a rescue centre in Kenya for girls fleeing FGM. The initiative is supported by British charity Equality Now, using funds from Comic Relief, and aims to educate Kenyan communities about FGM. Not only does it provide shelter for girls running away from their families and mediate in their reconciliation, but it also runs a very successful Alternate Rites of Passage project which carries out all the ceremony associated with the cutting but without the actual FGM itself. Since it started six years ago, it is estimated to have saved almost 1,500 girls from undergoing circumcision. Agnes is from a Maasai community and was cut herself, so no one is better placed to understand how to combat FGM in her region. She feels the project is a valuable way to preserve important elements of her culture, while abandoning the mutilation.

The programme has been designed for the Maasai community because different tribes practise FGM for different reasons, and something that works for one won't necessarily work for another.

Over a period of four days, the programme takes the girls and their mothers and teaches them everything that they would expect to learn from village elders after the cut – about reproduction, taking care of themselves and their family – but it also teaches the girls about the process of being cut, and that they don't need this to happen in order to be a woman.

The programme is working because the parents have been involved in its design – in fact, they often bring their girls to the Tasaru Ntomonok Initiative without active interference from the organisers. Agnes's charity also targets boys: 'When we talk boys through sex education, we tell them the importance of the clitoris; how if we interfere with the clitoris, we interfere with the pleasure,' explains Agnes. 'And when we tell them that, they are the first people to decide against FGM.'

Other strategies offered to FGM-practising communities include targeting the cutters themselves. Alternative income-generating schemes have become popular over the last few years, although opinions differ as to the effectiveness of these programmes, the suspicion being that some cutters simply take the new income but continue to cut. However, research carried out by 28 Too Many – a British charity set up to study FGM in the twenty-eight African countries where it is most prevalent – has discovered that, when combined with education to challenge belief, such initiatives can be a very successful way to turn people away from cutting.

'One of the things that reinforces FGM is that the people who traditionally carry it out are older women, and these women are very dependent on their role as cutters – it's how they get their status in the community and quite often it's how they earn their living as well,' explains Louise Robertson, the charity's communications manager. 'To break the cycle you need to get them to agree to stop cutting, but in order to do that you have to offer them another way of supporting themselves, otherwise they have no incentive to stop.' Often a 'soft loan', linked to animal husbandry – goats, chickens and rabbits – is provided. For example, a cutter may be given five goats and a ram – goats reproduce relatively quickly, so the cutter can sell the goats' milk and slaughter any extra animals to sell the meat, and eventually return to the scheme the number of goats she originally borrowed.

To reduce the likelihood of the cutters making use of the loans while continuing to cut, these schemes need to be integrated into the wider context of an overall programme, one that educates people about FGM and challenges the old beliefs. In Sierra Leone, a zero-tolerance policy was introduced, whereby a girl could no longer attend school if she had been cut, but it was felt by many that the wrong people were being punished. Now, in some parts of the country, an organisation called Masanga Education Assistance (MEA) has rolled out a programme in which Bondo women have committed to 'putting down their baskets', a symbolic giving-up of their cutting tools. Bondo is a secret all-female society that carries out and upholds age-old cultural traditions, their purpose being to help young women earn the rites of passage into womanhood. Their ceremonies take place in the Bondo bush, a private enclosure constructed near their village, and cutting has historically played an integral role in the transition. As part of the MEA's scheme, the

Bondo women continue to take the girls into the bush but they no longer do the cutting.

A number of projects have been established in various African countries, dedicated to finding alternatives to FGM while preserving cultural traditions. Given how firmly rooted it is within certain cultures, it is no wonder that health practitioners in Britain are concerned about the 173,000 girls, identified in a recent report, who have been born in the UK to women from FGM-practising countries.* The same report looked at the reasons behind the continuation of cutting here in the UK.

> In a number of communities, young women who do not undergo FGM may face stigma, discrimination and threats from family and community members ... A recurring theme for the justification of FGM in practising communities is to attenuate the sexual desire of females in order to conform to prescribed social norms relating to girls' and women's moral conduct. FGM is often linked to marriagability of girls and family 'honour'. A commonly held belief in FGM-practising communities is that girls and women who have not undergone FGM have an insatiable sexual appetite which has to be restrained to prevent bringing dishonour and shame to families.

My three daughters will have been among those 173,000 girls identified in that report, and yet they are safe because I decided

---

* Between 1996 and 2012, identified in the 2014 City University/Equality Now report.

that the practising of FGM within my family would end with me. There are many other mothers out there like me, who prioritised their child's safety and wellbeing, and their right to a body free from pain and infections. But despite the best intentions of some mothers, the cultural pressures prove stronger than their individual will. I have heard stories from my friends of their mothers doing everything they could to prevent their child from being cut and yet it was the wishes of the rest of the family that prevailed. One friend of mine remembers seeing her mother at the door, battling to get in as she herself was forced down on to the floor and cut. Imagine that mother's pain at seeing her child suffer the same as she had, and being physically restrained from trying to prevent the abuse.

Another FGM survivor who, like me, has asked herself many times how her mother could have subjected her to the practice is Fatuma Farah, who was cut in Somalia as a child and now lives and works in London as a psychotherapist, often working with women who have been cut. Much like my own story, Fatuma describes a loving mother who fiercely protected her daughter until she was cut at five. Fatuma came from a family of eight boys – as her parents' only daughter, she felt very much loved and cherished. As such, she found it even harder to understand how her mother could have allowed her to suffer such an abuse, but it only goes to illustrate how deeply ingrained the practice is.

My mum passed away two years ago and it was always a sore point between us even until the end. I cared for her in the last three months before her death and we had a lot of conversations. My mum was a very lovely and caring woman and she apologised for all the mistakes she'd made, but she never apologised for the FGM. Until her dying day she didn't think she'd done anything wrong. My mother was illiterate and she didn't have any education, and she thought wrongly that it was a religious requirement. She also didn't have the medical knowledge to know or understand the complications of it. Of course she knew there was a lot of pain involved, but she didn't know any better. As far as she was concerned, she'd had it, her mother had it, everyone around her was having it and I would have it.

Fatuma is sure that had her father been around more when she was that age instead of out at work, he would have convinced her mother not to have her cut. 'He was more educated than my mother, he would have spoken to her and said don't do it.' As I've explained, men were often absent from the daily run of things, it was very common in Somalian households at that time. However, unlike Fatuma, even if there had been more input from my father, I am not convinced that it would have made a difference because men traditionally see *gudnin* as women's business. For that reason, they turn a blind eye because they tell themselves that it doesn't concern them. Just like other aspects of child-rearing, there are certain men who are happy to leave it to women, and because they don't concern themselves with FGM, they never talk to women about it.

When I recently gave a talk to a packed town-hall meeting in

CUT

north-east London, I didn't expect any husbands or fathers to turn up, so I was amazed when I walked in and found sixty men waiting patiently to hear about a subject they'd long avoided. One of them was forty-two-year-old Abbas. Like most of the men there, he didn't know what to expect when he'd walked into the room, perhaps wall-to-wall women, and yet every single chair was taken up by a man. One of the reasons Abbas had been persuaded to attend was because, as well as having three sons, he had a nine-year-old daughter, and he felt this talk might be relevant to him. He hadn't had his little girl cut, not because he thought the practice was bad – he hadn't given it too much thought before – but mostly because it appeared to him to be old-fashioned.

However, what he heard in that room that night, during the talk I gave, would change the way he thought about FGM forever.

I didn't know until that talk about the medical problems. I didn't know about the side effects, and I didn't think that this was still practised a lot. FGM is not something that we talk to other Somalians about. Men don't speak about women's problems in our culture; it's not something you have an open conversation about, not even within your own family.

Telling a roomful of Somalian men exactly what FGM was, I watched as realisation dawned on each of their faces. I saw them swallow hard when I used words like 'clitoris' and 'vagina', words that are not shared between men and women in our culture. But if

174

FGM is carried out in the name of men, isn't it important that we hear what they have to say?

Abbas describes how most Somalian men first encounter the practice:

> I was very young, maybe eight or ten years old, when I first heard of FGM. It wasn't called that in Somalia, it was called *gudnin*. As a young boy you can't help but notice when your neighbours go through it, or your sisters ...
>
> You don't question it because everyone does it; it is the norm and if you don't do it you are different to the rest of the people. You are brainwashed about this idea, they make you believe that if girls don't go through this then they are different, they are not normal girls, they are not good girls. That's the only point of carrying out FGM, to protect her virginity until she gets married. It could be to stop the woman from having sex with a man, or stop the man from having sex with her, but old cultures don't hold a man accountable; they're instead always looking at women's actions. I thought it was unfair and way out of date, but this was the seventies. I left Somalia for London in the nineties and I'm forty-two now. I didn't think anyone was still doing it.

Abbas's acknowledgement of the fact that he thought of FGM as simply a 'woman's problem' is a sentiment that is repeated by many men, and it is exactly this mindset that means men play their part in allowing this practice to continue, simply by not asking any questions.

I didn't know until your talk that it was [not prescribed by] religion. I didn't know because I wasn't interested that much, I was just neutral. I wasn't saying no, and I wasn't saying yes; I didn't have good evidence to dismiss it or good evidence to accept it. I was standing in the middle of this argument, but when I heard it from your point of view and from a cleric who said from a religious point of view it's not right, I was amazed.

I took the cleric, a friend of Yusuf's, along with me for that reason, to tell the men who were there that this was not a religious practice, it was a cultural one. I have always found it impossible to understand how people who believe in God think that He would have created something imperfect, that we need to slice bits off girls because God didn't create the female of the species properly the first time round. But there was no point in me telling people that; they needed to hear it from a religious person, and as Mohamed Abdulle spoke, I saw the men look up and pay closer attention. They really were learning something new.

Abbas also had no idea about the side effects that women suffer. He had no idea about the medical complications or the problems that can occur when giving birth. He had grown up, just like me, in a culture where FGM was so ingrained as a belief that nobody thought to question it, and, also like me, he thought that he'd left these 'old-fashioned' practices behind in Somalia. He had no idea that they had reached British shores.

I spoke to other men and everyone understood that something needs to be done, the reaction was very positive. It would be good if men stood up together and said, 'Don't do this for us.' If we stood up and said no then it would stop. Women are doing this practice thinking that it is for men, but if we marched, if we signed petitions, if we went on television and told them that we don't want FGM then maybe that would take the pressure off women.

I agree with Abbas: until men stand up against FGM and say, 'I do not want this done to girls in my name', the practice will continue. While men accept the practice thinking that women want it, women will do it thinking that men want it – this is what UNICEF referred to in a 2013 report as 'pluralistic ignorance'.* That's why men are absolutely key to ending FGM.

Fatuma Farah used to work for the Ministry of Health in Somalia, and in her role there, she met a male doctor who was mobilising a group of men to go marching, to make it clear that they did not want little girls to be mutilated in their name. 'I really do believe that had it happened, a big shift would have taken place,' Farah told me, 'but men didn't want to do it; they said it was a big shame in their culture to talk about women's genitals. I still believe it would have a huge impact on FGM if men stood up and marched and said no to it. And it's very achievable.'

There have been other more successful instances of men taking

* 'Female Genital Mutilation/Cutting: A statistical overview and exploration of the dynamics of change', UNICEF, 2013.

a stand. There are thought to be more than one million cricket teams across the world – but there is only one Maasai team. The men compete in traditional dress, bowling in their *shuka* shawls and scoring runs while ornately decorated with colourful beaded headdresses. They look quite striking as they hit fours and sixes, and yet the message they deliver through their game is equally inspiring: end FGM. These young men are Maasai warriors, each of them between seventeen and twenty-two, an age when most of them would traditionally be ready for marriage. Instead, they are on a mission to convince their village elders to end the barbaric practice that has blighted the lives of young girls in their community for generations, via the game of cricket. These boys live in a remote tribe in the shadow of Mount Kenya. In their community, it is customary to cut girls at around the age of eleven or twelve. And once a girl has been cut, she is ready for marriage, which means she must also abandon her education.

Benjamin and Daniel are two of these Maasai warrior-cricketers. Their younger sister, Nancy, works hard at school – so hard, in fact, that she won a scholarship to study at an American secondary school in Kenya. When the time came for her to be cut and married off among her tribe, her brothers could not stand by and watch her education and her life be destroyed by FGM. Benjamin and Daniel managed to persuade their parents not to have Nancy cut and to let her continue her studies, but they received threats of physical violence from other members of their community as a result of speaking out. The brothers' mission wasn't just to save Nancy, it was to save other girls too, and so they turned to a British charity called Cricket Without Boundaries (CWB) to help them with their cause.

CWB was founded in the UK ten years ago and is primarily an HIV and AIDS awareness charity. Its aim is to teach boys and girls in African communities how to play cricket, alongside delivering valuable educational messages. They'd been working with the Maasai Cricket Warriors for seven or eight years, but this was the first time that the charity had been asked to deliver an anti-FGM message. 'The boys had gained status in their community through cricket,' says Hannah Weaver, chief executive of the charity. 'It made them stars in their tribe, and it gave them the voice and the confidence to speak out. That's the power of sport. But we knew that FGM was extremely culturally sensitive and we had to think long and hard about how we could make it work and deliver the project, while attempting to limit as much potential kick-back on the boys as possible.' CWB enrolled the help of 28 Too Many and Hannah went out to Kenya to deliver the first programme in early 2015.

> When we're teaching communities about AIDS, we use cricket as a metaphor – we explain how important it is to protect yourself and your stumps in the game of cricket, and then liken that to protecting yourself by wearing a condom. We had to come up with similar analogies in the context of FGM, so we created the acronym 'BAT'. 'B' stood for 'breaking the silence', and we likened it to how you have to use your voice in cricket – you have to call the ball and say, 'It's mine', and you have to talk to

179

your team-mates. The message was that if we break the silence of FGM then we can beat it. 'A' stood for 'advocate of change', so we talked about how in a game of cricket you change your game according to what's happening with the ball. And 'T' stood for 'team together' – how working as a team in cricket makes you stronger, and how tackling FGM is not something you can do in isolation.

The programme also enabled boys and girls to play the sport together, which in turn opened up a conversation about FGM between them, allowing for a lot of myths to be debunked, according to Hannah.

It was really surprising to hear twelve- or thirteen-year-old boys saying that a girl had to be cut because if she wasn't she would have lots of sex and won't be tame. When we women stood up and told girls in classes that we ran charities, or we were midwives, or we were engineers and we weren't cut, you heard them gasp. One girl even asked me if I had to 'wrap' myself – she thought that if you didn't cut the clitoris it just grew longer and longer.

If these beliefs exist in this new generation of young boys, you can imagine the perceptions of men two generations before them. Mohamed is fifty-nine years old and came to live in Britain twenty years ago. He has been married for twenty-five years and has four sons:

I did think it was a good idea when I was a young man. It is some kind of guarantee. When you go to a shop and you buy something you get a warranty; that's the view I had in those days, that my wife being cut was my guarantee that she was a virgin, you know that no other man has touched her. Now I'm a grown man I realise it is just an idea; whether she was touched or not it doesn't make any difference. From the point of view of the woman, even if she wasn't touched by a man before you, she could still commit adultery afterwards; it makes no sense. Looking back, it was a mixture of good and bad. The good was that you didn't have to concern yourself that anybody had touched your wife before you; the bad side is seeing your wife suffer and complain about being in pain when you are intimate. I didn't like it then; there was no pleasure in the bedroom for the first month. I felt pressure on me too. I wanted to do something about it for her – maybe some kind of lubricant – but there was nothing I could do. As a man you won't even enjoy yourself in the bed; you can't ignore it if your wife is complaining of pain. But as a man you don't go out and speak about these things, not even to a doctor. You just suffer silently.

Of course, you can't compare a man's suffering – his lack of sexual enjoyment – with how a woman has suffered due to FGM, but just as Mohamed confesses, the experience isn't good for either party. So would he want his sons to marry a woman who has been cut? He says he wouldn't talk to them about such things, a hangover from the secrecy surrounding the subject back in Somalia, but it's also true that parents the world over find it uncomfortable talking to their children about intimate matters. However, from his own experiences it seems he wouldn't encourage them to.

> I don't think my sons will marry girls who are cut, they were born in this country. I tell them they can marry whoever they want. Children born here have a different attitude, and their perception is different according to the British laws. Men have to stand up and say we don't want this – if the father figure stands up then the mother won't do anything to the child.

Dr Comfort Momoh runs an FGM clinic at St Thomas' Hospital in London but has travelled around FGM-prevalent countries and observed many different attitudes in men. She maintains that it is important not to generalise the opinions of men, as they can differ just as women's experiences of FGM can differ. However, what does seem to recur is the fact that, while men are aware of FGM, they don't have an insight into what actually happens. Most of the men are not involved in the celebration or the cutting – it is the realm of the women, and the women take ownership because to their minds they are preparing their daughter for adulthood and marriage. 'If men as the head of the family make a stand and say, "I don't want my daughter to have FGM", things will change,' she says. 'But at the moment, men are saying, "It's got nothing to do with me, it's a woman's problem." They need to get involved.'

How exactly? What is the best way of engaging men in a topic that they have shied away from for generations? Solomon Zewolde is a researcher at the charity FORWARD UK. He is working along-side fellow researchers in Belgium and Holland on a project called Men Speak Out. The three-year research project started in January 2015, and aims to recruit fifteen peer educators in each country to go out into communities and speak to men and women. Solomon grew up in Ethiopia and moved to Britain four years ago. He had experience of FGM in the community in which he grew up and knew of relatives, friends and neighbours who had been cut.

One of the myths told about uncut women is that they will be ill-mannered, that they will misbehave if they are not cut; they need to be cut so they behave well and appear decent, which will make them suitable for marriage and sought-after. We should never be under the illusion that women are consenting to this harm being done or that women are perpetuating the practice because they need it – that is simply not true. As in everything else, the oppression against women appears to be something women accept but that's not the case. Patriarchal societies all over the world have made women submit to certain practices. This is submission, not consent, and we need to make a distinction between the two.

Over three years, the Men Speak Out initiative will conduct focus groups and surveys to find out more about the issues and concerns men have. Solomon believes the first difficulty that needs to be overcome is getting men to acknowledge that an FGM problem both abroad and in Britain even exists.

Some would like to deny that it exists. There is a lack of knowledge; there's a lot of ignorance of what FGM is, what the cut is, about the medical consequences, the social consequences, the psychological consequences . . . In research I ask them, 'Do you know exactly what the cut is?' Most think it's OK, that it's just a little prick. They say, 'Why are you making a big fuss about this?' I think attitudes will change once we fill that gap of knowledge. When men know the different types of FGM – that there's not just one type – and the severity of it, if we have medical professionals talking to them about the consequences and have some survivors coming out and telling them what they've been through, how horrible it is and how it stays with them throughout their life – even when they are cut at a very early age – I can see people beginning to change. Education is key, along with the law.

Until men stand up against FGM, women may be encouraged to continue the practice because they will still be concerned that their daughter won't find a husband. In some cultures, being cut or uncut affects every aspect of their daughter's life: her acceptance by society, her marriageability and therefore her future. That is why Solomon's project is so important – we need to galvanise men to speak out and reassure mothers that their daughters won't be disadvantaged if they are not cut.

It is difficult to understand why women, when they know the pain involved, continue the practice. Then, when you hear stories like Mohamed's, who saw how his wife suffered, you wonder equally how fathers could decide to put their daughters through that. When I put this to Solomon, that surely witnessing for themselves the pain women suffer must make men want to turn away from the practice, he told me about a darker side of FGM that has come to light through the research project.

> One of my colleagues in Holland was told by a Somalian man in a focus group discussion that he feels more pleasure when his wife feels more pain. He told them that he feels more masculine, more happy, the more pain she feels. I honestly believe that he represents a significant number of people in many countries who believe that putting a woman through pain during sex makes them feel more masculine.

Solomon believes that this is connected to wider issues which affect communities all over the world who don't discuss sex – even between couples. He feels that if this taboo subject was discussed more, how each partner could receive more pleasure during sex, attitudes like this would change.

For every man like the one Solomon describes, there are also men, like Mohamed, who take no pleasure in seeing their wife suffer. And sadly, a common story that Solomon has heard is of the men who divorce or cheat on wives who have been cut because they don't have a fulfilling sex life. Remember that men are not encouraged to save themselves for sex after marriage, so a man knows that a different sex life is available to him out there.

This to me is the double abuse that women often suffer. A man can dump his wife for not sexually satisfying him because sex is very painful for her because of the cut or because, in some cultures, a woman might be opened and closed, and opened and closed at different milestones like after giving birth. So she denies him, and he in turn divorces her or dumps her at home and goes out and has sex with uncut women. That is not uncommon, and yet again she suffers through no fault of her own. People never talk about this. They camouflage it and instead give many other reasons for the break-up of a marriage – no one will tell you it's because of bad sexual experiences.

In that case, FGM is actually breaking down family units. The premise of it, somewhere very far back, was surely to prevent adultery (at least on the woman's part), and yet accounts of FGM being the cause of adultery or divorce are very common. I myself have lived with this fear my whole married life, despite having a husband who is devoted to me; when your body has let you down you feel like you are less of a woman, you worry that you won't be enough for your man.

Educating men about FGM is clearly a very good thing indeed and definitely the way forward, but there is still the worry that modern men – particularly those in Britain – who have already turned their backs on the practice may then also reject girls who've been cut. Solomon has a strong message for men about that.

Education is the first place but the message has to be to stand up against the cut, not against the cut *woman*. This is a very important message. Say no, you can't cut girls, but we don't want men to stand against girls who have already been cut; we want men to stand with them, to try to help these women who are having problems. Men play a very decisive role in ending this practice. The important thing is to root the belief and commitment in them that it really needs to stop, and that requires a lot of education and a lot of effort, but it is possible.

We need to bring men on board to work alongside women, for men and women to stand shoulder to shoulder in the fight to end this practice both in African and Middle Eastern countries as well as in the UK.

15

A Very British Problem

According to the City University London/Equality Now report published in 2014, with every decade that passes, FGM becomes even more of a British problem. In 2001, it was estimated that there were 66,000 women aged fifteen to forty-nine living in England and Wales who were born in countries where FGM was widely practised. By 2011, that figure had swollen to 103,000.*

Twenty-one women out of every 1,000 are victims of FGM in London. In towns like Milton Keynes, Cardiff, Coventry, Sheffield, Reading, Thurrock, Northampton and Oxford, seven females in every 1,000 are victims. In rural areas, fewer than one in 1,000 women are living with FGM, but that's still more than

* 'Prevalence of Female Genital Mutilation in England and Wales: National and local estimates', Alison Macfarlane, City University London/Equality Now, 2014.

zero. Researchers came up with these estimates based on the 2011 census, migration figures and surveys of how prevalent FGM is in those countries from which women have migrated. The numbers could be lower, of course, but they could also be much higher.

More accurate statistics are perhaps those provided by health professionals in Britain. In 2015, the government released figures of actual cases of FGM that had been recorded over a five-month period.* Doctors, nurses and healthcare professionals were asked to keep the first record of the number of new women and girls presenting to them with symptoms of FGM, and those being treated for ongoing problems. There are thousands of women being identified as victims of FGM every single year in Britain. Between September 2014 and January 2015, more than 2,600 new cases of FGM were identified. Forty-four of those were children under eighteen. More than 9,500 women were deinfibulated. And remember, these are only the women and girls who have sought medical treatment – many more must be suffering in silence.

As Halima's story shows, such is the pressure within FGM-practising communities in Britain to maintain traditions that, despite the fact that FGM has been illegal in the UK since 1985 and that, since 2003, it is against the law to take UK nationals out of the country to be cut, parents will risk prosecution and return with their children to their homelands in order for them to be mutilated. Back in 2013, when my head teacher and I were faced with the obvious truth that Halima's parents were planning

* 'Female Genital Mutilation (FGM) January 2015, experimental statistics', Health and Social Care Information Centre, 27 February 2015.

exactly this, we were frustratingly helpless to do anything other than plead with them not to take her out of school in term time. But new legislation introduced in England, Wales and Northern Ireland in 2015 meant that one woman was able to protect her three daughters from FGM in Britain just hours after that change in the law came into effect.

Funke was a survivor of FGM, which was carried out when she was in her teens at the request of the family of the man she would be forced to marry back in Nigeria. She was forced to undergo the Type 2 procedure, and had her clitoris and labia removed against her will. The wounds never properly healed, and would usually open up again after sexual intercourse, causing her horrific pain each time. Given her suffering, she was adamant that her daughters, who were aged twelve, nine and six, would not experience the same agony. Her children were born in Nigeria, but have had British residency since Funke divorced their father and moved with them to the UK. She was well aware that her ex-husband, who has a history of violence, had always been keen to get the girls cut. Early in 2015, he started applying pressure on her via telephone calls and texts from Nigeria, demanding that the girls undergo circumcision. Funke knew her ex-husband viewed mutilating the girls as both 'inevitable and necessary' and, despite the fact that FGM was outlawed in Nigeria in May 2015, he ordered Funke to prepare the girls for travel in the summer holidays.

Here, in a family court transcript, as she made a request to the judge to ban the girls' father from cutting them, she describes what she was up against.

191

In February 2015, he sent the ceremonial robes from Nigeria in preparation for [the cutting]. Now the school holiday is upon us he has told me, via messages, that he expects to see the children immediately. He has requested that the two elder girls be sent now. He is angry because the eldest is over ten years old and past the usual age for the procedure to happen . . .

She goes on to describe how he also requested the umbilical cords and first teeth of the children to be used as part of the ceremony. Upon hearing her testimony, the judge granted Funke a FGM Protection Order. This is a civil measure that can be requested by either the female in jeopardy, a relevant third party or any other person with the permission of the court, which offers protection to victims and potential victims of FGM, the breach of which is a criminal offence. The order came into effect immediately, and was then served on their father in Nigeria, along with injunctions that stopped him coming within 100 metres of the girls' mother, their home or their school.

The situation that Funke found herself in is far from uncommon – there must have been thousands of mothers before her who were desperate to protect their daughters but lacked the knowledge, resources and, until 2015, law to make it happen. However, just as the legal system adapts to try to protect children like Funke's daughters, the face of FGM in Britain is also changing to evade it. With the price of airline tickets soaring, families in the UK are now holding what are referred to as 'FGM parties', whereby relatives can avoid the cost of sending a group of girls back to villages where they will be cut by clubbing together to pay the cost of one single village cutter to travel to the UK instead.

Imagine the scene: in a suburban living room in Bristol, eight girls line up alongside their cousins. They are not sure why, but a buzz of excitement has been building all week. They are wearing special clothes which have been bought for the occasion, and their favourite foods have filled the family home for days. Their extended families have gathered, and everyone seems happy. The girls don't know what is about to take place, or who the strange woman with wrinkled hands is, although she seems to be someone of great importance, and each of their parents makes a point of thanking her in turn for undertaking the journey alone. All the eight girls understand is that whatever is about to happen to them will prepare them for being a woman. An hour later the living room smells of fear and blood, and hot tears streak the girls' faces, as the stranger wreaks havoc on their young bodies with the razor blades their parents have bought for the job.

The cutter herself will be on a plane home before there is any chance of her being detected, her bags heavy with the money that exchanged hands for her trouble. After all, an elderly woman travelling alone, claiming to be visiting family, would be no cause for concern to Border Agency staff. With the cutting done at the beginning of the summer holidays, by the time the girls are fit and recovered enough to return to school in September, the last thing they will want to do is alert anyone and go over the awful events of that day. Instead, they say nothing, and neither do their parents, and another case of FGM in Britain goes unprosecuted.

Families have changed tack now that the authorities have cottoned on to the practice of taking girls out of the country to be cut, intercepting them before they can make the journey abroad. Instead, girls are being cut in living rooms up and down the country. Such is the secrecy of this practice that it goes undetected, until, that is, a girl shows up years later in an antenatal ward, pregnant herself, when it is impossible to tell when – let alone where or how – she was cut, and at which stage she's unlikely to want to see her parents jailed for their actions, or to rake up the past that they have long buried. And so it continues.

It is, of course, impossible to get anyone to go on record with firm evidence of these FGM parties. There are rumours of them in any community where families have been practising FGM for generations, but the minute the police press anyone for further details about who is involved and what takes place and where, all conversations are shut down. No one will give specific details; they only insist time and time again that it happens.

This is the problem that the police, social services and healthcare workers in the UK face constantly. Aniso was a young teenage girl living with her mother in London, in neglectful conditions. Her relationship with her mother had broken down and so she contacted social services. She was placed with a foster family and went on to tell the welfare officers that she had been a victim of FGM and that it had been arranged by her mother. An investigation by the Metropolitan Police and social services was opened immediately, and after interviews, it was agreed that there was enough evidence to bring the first criminal case against FGM since the legislation was passed in 1985. But during the investigation, presumably when officers told Aniso they were ready to prosecute her mother, she changed her mind and refused to co-operate with police. She told them she feared the community would ostracise her if she testified against her mother in court.

The officers were perplexed: she'd come to them to report this, and she'd seemed happy to give a statement when their investigation started. They tried to convince her to change her mind, offering her support from both the police and third-sector agencies, and impressed on her the importance of standing up to a practice that amounted to child abuse. But Aniso refused; she told them that if they made her go to court she would kill herself.

The officers, who had spent many man-hours on the case, were left with no other choice but to abandon it, and the paperwork was placed at the back of a file, another potential prosecution lost to them. Unfortunately, this is not an unfamiliar story for the law-enforcement agencies. Girls and young women refusing to testify against their parents is one of the major reasons why there has not been one single successful prosecution in thirty years.

However, this does not mean that the police are not trying to change this situation. Since 2012, the Crown Prosecution Service (CPS) has decided that no further action should be taken on thirteen cases of FGM that the police have brought before them.* That's thirteen files, all those man-hours, all those officers, all those statements and, most importantly, thirteen children who

---

* Source: CPS via email.

have not had any justice for the child abuse that was carried out on them. Imagine all the other cases that came before 2012 which were also dismissed.

Too often the finger of blame is pointed at the police for not having secured any successful prosecutions, and, given this fact, some have questioned whether FGM is even a problem in Britain today. Sadly, this isn't the case. I spoke to a detective who has been investigating child abuse for the last eleven years. She works as part of the Metropolitan Police's Project Azure, a specialist unit set up to investigate incidents of FGM in London.

> If we take a case to court, we have to prove beyond reasonable doubt that someone is guilty. We know FGM exists, but as police officers we deal in evidence and we often have none. Much of the information we receive is anecdotal. It's very frustrating. It's like all child abuse – children will tell you they're being sexually abused because they want it to stop, not because they want their parents prosecuted. Your mum is still your mum.

I can understand that more than anyone. Given the chance, would I have seen my mum sent to prison for what she allowed to happen to me? Would I have testified against her and seen her taken from the family home, and with her everything I'd ever known? No. As much as I hated her for what she did, as great as the damage it did to our relationship, I wouldn't have wanted to condemn her to prison. And it's those kinds of mixed feelings that the police investigating teams are faced with each day. Add to that the fact that many children might not even know they have been victims of abuse, particularly if they were cut as a baby and have no recollection of it at all. To suddenly make that leap from thinking you'd grown up in a completely loving family to the notion of your parents being child abusers is a difficult, if not sometimes impossible, transition.

Project Azure detectives work with many 'community champions' – advisers who act as a 'go-between' for the community and officials – who tell them that FGM is happening in the UK, but when questioned further for more detail they are met with a closed door and no amount of pushing will gain access to further information. Without evidence, the police are unable to arrest anyone – and the person they want to arrest is the cutter, not a poor, uneducated mother who may not realise that the practice is illegal in this country. This, sadly, is the situation facing UK police forces across the country.

These detectives recognise that FGM is a complex issue. Not only is there a lack of people willing to testify and a veil of silence surrounding the abuse, but it's not always clear who the perpetrator is. Some mothers are entirely against FGM but their relatives carry it out regardless, sometimes without the mother's knowledge. Who should be prosecuted in such instances? 'If a person were to travel back to their country of origin, that child might not be at risk from their family, but from the wider community,' explains one detective. 'We know of stories where parents have found out their children have been cut unbeknownst to them – that must be devastating. The communities that practise it might not even know that what they have done is against the law in the UK, and that's why education is paramount.'

Notwithstanding all these difficulties, the police continue in their attempts to act on any case of FGM that is brought to their attention, whether the CPS decides to pursue it or not, and to focus on the goal of prevention and not just on prosecution. Since 2009, a flag is raised at Project Azure whenever an incident is reported to the Metropolitan Police that has even a suspicion of FGM, which means that detectives monitor the prevalence of FGM across London, and pass on information to the relevant authorities to make enquiries. Since 2014, FGM training has become mandatory for first-response officers in the Met. The number of flags made to Project Azure is rising, and hopefully this is down to the greater number of officers who have been educated about what female circumcision is and what they need to look out for. The police have been working with social services on drawing up safeguarding arrangements, contributing to local-authority assessments that might result in a child being removed from a high-risk situation and confiscating passports from families to prevent them from travelling abroad. 'We would rather a thousand children were pro-tected rather than one person prosecuted, even though our job is to investigate,' says another detective. 'We always say that prevention is better than cure. We do a lot of small talks to training groups and big talks at conferences. And if you've spoken to a group of thirty people and you see the lightbulbs start flashing as you educate them about FGM, you know that while you may not have directly protected a child that day, you've spoken to people who can.'

As well as training police officers, detectives from Project Azure liaise with community projects, the Department for Education, the Department of Health and of course the Home Office, advising them on what protocols will help support and identify victims of FGM. They also work with the Border Agency at airports, speaking with and educating people who have arrived on flights from countries where FGM is prevalent, in case they have been cut and are in need of support – though, of course, it is not necessarily easy to identify a girl who may or may not have been cut – or in case they could identify a cutter, although that is also a near-impossible task.

Recently the law was changed, making it mandatory to report any suspicions of FGM to the police. This means that any health or social-care professional – including doctors, who must usually abide by doctor-patient confidentiality – or teacher who hears of a cutting taking place has a legal duty to report it as a crime. However, this has met with some resistance, the concern being that it might deter women from seeking medical assistance, for fear that there will be wider repercussions as a result. But other amendments have been made to the Serious Crime Act, such as extending protection to both British and non-British citizens, providing anonymity to victims, and making it the duty of any person who is responsible for the girl (defined as those having 'frequent contact') to protect her from FGM, with a possible prison term of seven years for failure to do so. Certainly, the greatest move towards ensuring the protection of children at risk of FGM in Britain has been the introduction of the FGM Protection Order that Funke was able to request.

CUT

This new civil legislation was spearheaded by London family-law barrister Zimran Samuel and his colleagues, many of whom worked pro bono. It was after watching *The Cruel Cut*, a documentary on FGM, that Zimran decided to take up the cause. Along with human-rights barrister Dexter Dias QC, Zimran submitted some recommendations to a parliamentary inquiry that was reviewing legislation on FGM, which included the idea of the FGM Protection Order – a piece of legislation that wouldn't necessarily result in criminal prosecutions, but which would allow girls themselves to seek protection. Zimran approached the issue from the angle of a family lawyer, aware of the sensitivities and concerns that can surround any action pursued by the police and social services.

> The main issue was that girls were often not coming forward because they didn't want their parents to go to prison, and the criminal law is a blunt instrument. So we evolved an idea taken from the work I do within cases of forced marriage and recommended FGM Protection Orders as an amendment to the FGM Act of 2003. Normally, in the family court cases, those under eighteen need the permission of the court to apply for an order, but with these orders girls can apply themselves, even girls who are under eighteen. The scope of the people who can apply to protect the girl on her behalf is wide, too, as long as you can prove you are a connected person – a sister who has heard her younger sibling is going to be cut, for example, or a mother, a father, a teacher or even a friend. We just need to encourage girls

200

to come forward and let them know that the route to protect themselves or others is not only prosecution.

The FGM Protection Order allows a judge to take out an injunction to stop the cutting from taking place. It also automatically triggers a liaison between professionals: police, social services, doctors. Providing there is evidence that a girl is about to be cut, obtaining an order is relatively easy – it can be done over the phone to a judge by a lawyer and out of hours, and it offers immediate protection for the girl, even if she's already out of the country.

Within forty-eight hours of this new legislation coming into force, Zimran had already obtained an FGM Protection Order to safeguard Funke's three children. Commencement of the new legislation was brought forward to time with the school holidays which started on 17 July 2015 – although there was no opportunity to roll out a huge awareness campaign about it (and, in fact, the family lawyer Funke had originally approached found Zimran on Twitter, of all places). The most important thing is that those three girls are now protected. That, to me, is huge progress. However, Zimran warns there is still more work to do.

Until the last two years, doctors and teachers and social workers weren't really talking about FGM – they saw it as a Somalian or Nigerian issue, and that just isn't the case. It is a British issue. I think we've been far too cautious as a nation and I think that there are a lot of lessons to be learned from France, which has been dealing with this problem very well since the early nineties.

There is no better example of just what a problem FGM is for teachers than the story of Sayfiya. In August 2015, Miss Smith, a secondary-school teacher, was busy preparing her classroom for the new term. She had chosen that particular day to go into school purely at random and, despite the fact that it was the school holidays and she should have been enjoying a well-deserved break, she decided to check her work email. What she found there sent shivers down her spine. It was an email from one of her thirteen-year-old students, a young girl called Sayfiya, who was bright, articulate and hard-working. Except she wasn't enjoying her summer holidays like her friends. Instead, she had been taken with her brother against her will to Sudan – a country where 88 per cent of women undergo FGM. A country where women are not just sewn up in preparation for marriage, but are often restitched each time they give birth. The last two words on the end of the desperate message to her teacher read: 'Please help'.

Miss Smith immediately contacted the police, who informed the Foreign Office, and negotiations began with the Sudanese authorities to try to locate Sayfiya and her brother and bring them home. Her mother, who had returned to the UK without her children, had undergone FGM as a child, along with her sisters. She had talked in the past about cutting her own daughter, so there was a strong suspicion that this young girl was about to be mutilated too. Barristers in the UK had no time to waste and – under the instruction of Kent Children's Services in conjunction with the Foreign Office – immediately secured an FGM Protection Order.

Two things make this case particularly remarkable – and

worrying. Firstly, it was their own mother – a woman described as 'middle class' living in an affluent Kent suburb – who had allegedly abducted the children and taken them to Sudan, against their father's wishes. Sayfiya had already gone as far as tearing up her passport in an attempt to stay in Britain with her school friends and everything that was familiar to her. However, her mother had simply obtained another, such was her determination that her daughter should move to a country where child marriage is legal.

The second thing that makes this story unique is that the passports they held were British ones; these two children had been born in this country and were British citizens. They knew nothing of the life they were about to be introduced to. What they knew was British streets and British television, pop stars and after-school clubs. For them, Sudan was an unfamiliar country with an unfamiliar culture. Thankfully, the FGM Protection Order offered Sayfiya a guarantee of safety, and she was returned home safely to the UK. But can you imagine how afraid Sayfiya must have felt? To be taken from all that is familiar to her and dumped in Sudan; to exchange the life she knows in Britain for an alien country. To live in a place where practices that are illegal here and viewed as barbaric are not only accepted but she will now be subjected to them. It is stories like these that make me want to fight to educate every single schoolchild about the risks. Sayfiya is clearly a bright girl; she raised the alarm by contacting her schoolteacher and in turn her teacher knew how to respond.

As Zimran notes, other countries have taken a more hardline approach to FGM and have achieved results when it comes to prosecutions. In the past thirty-five years, there have been at least twenty-nine trials in France, resulting in 100 people – both parents and cutters – being convicted. In France, schoolgirls are subjected to mandatory examinations, and some people in the UK – including the Labour MP Diane Abbott – have called for the same in this country, saying we have been too tolerant in the past. 'We do not need simple consciousness-raising and educational information. We have to face up to the need for prosecution and for routine medical examination,' Abbott said in 2014, during a parliamentary debate on FGM. 'It is a practice to which some of the British authorities have turned a blind eye for too long. It is long overdue that we, as a political class, take serious action on FGM.'*

While I agree that we have engaged in wilful blindness, I don't agree with forcing girls to have their genitals examined by the state. These girls and women will already have been through the trauma of being cut; they will feel isolated, ashamed, freakish – all the things that I felt when I arrived in this country. To make them open their legs to be forcibly examined by a stranger would, in my opinion, be a violation of their human rights – even if it did result in more prosecutions. And even then, who is to say there would be a guilty verdict? Both Zimran and I believe that what we need instead is a continued conversation about FGM, more support available for women to seek out, more resources ploughed into educating people about it.

* http://www.standard.co.uk/news/london/diane-abott-calls-for-mandatory-checks-on-schoolgirls-to-secure-prosecutions-for-fgm-9184171.html

Criminal law has its own place and I'm keen to see prosecutions against the cutters, but I'd rather focus on prevention. We need to go further; we need to train judges so that they know the high-risk areas and how to talk to victims. In the Foreign Office we have a Forced Marriage Unit, offering training for professionals up and down the country; it offers a helpline girls can call any time, day or night, with full-time staff. Most importantly, it liaises with foreign embassies around the world to repatriate girls who are at risk. That doesn't exist for FGM; there is a similar unit in the Home Office but it doesn't have the same clout, the same staff, or the same liaisons with different countries. In name it is similar, but in hours and resources and staff it is completely different. Its focus tends to be FGM within the UK. However, there is now an FGM lead within the Forced Marriage Unit, which continues to do incredible work on the frontline.

I agree with Zimran wholeheartedly, that the protection needs to be extended and maximised. These new laws and amendments to existing legislation all contribute to giving girls in the UK the right to refuse to be cut. But it's not just British citizens who need to be protected. Dexter Dias QC has championed the broadening of the legal protection offered to cover non-permanent residents as well.

It is a question of how genuine we are about implementing the human rights treaties that we are signed up to. Children who are on these shores – no matter where they come from – should have equal protection. Our obligations under the UN convention, which we are signatories to, say that we have a duty to protect all children. It is an absurdity that we might not protect a child who has only just arrived in this country and is then sent back to Somalia to be mutilated and that the adults involved have not committed a criminal offence. Whereas it *is* a criminal offence if the same thing happens to a child who has been here for a few more weeks and is therefore 'settled'. We have a duty under international law to provide real support and real financial commitment to ending harmful practices where women and children are the subject of physical harm and discrimination, and FGM is one of the most egregious examples of both things. We have a duty to engage with communities and get them collectively to move away from these practices.

But we can only do that – only fulfil our duties – if the British public stops looking away, because the more we pretend these things aren't happening (just like I did for years), the more they will continue in secrecy. We must protect children – all children – from abuse; there can be no ifs or buts.

16

The Medicalisation of FGM

I n 2013, the NSPCC set out to discover just what British teachers knew about FGM. Their findings made for some pretty
depressing reading: 16 per cent said they didn't know that FGM
was a crime, despite the fact that it has been illegal in this country
for thirty years.* Another 16 per cent said they didn't consider FGM
child abuse. And 60 per cent were not aware of any government
guidance on how they should tackle suspected cases. A massive
83 per cent of them also said they had received no adequate FGM
training. There are initiatives that are trying to change this picture,
but it is deeply worrying that there is still a lack of training and
awareness among teachers about the true horror of FGM. And if

* http://www.theguardian.com/teacher-network/teacher-blog/2013/jul/23/protect-
students-female-genital-mutilation

such a knowledge gap exists among educated individuals who interact daily with children from a multitude of migrant communities, what must we assume about the ignorance of the wider British public?

Some 60,000 children who are at risk are going to school each day where their caregiver might have no idea what FGM is or how to deal with it. What would a teacher say if a child confessed to them that they had been cut during the school holidays, or that they feared they might be taken abroad at half term to a country they'd never visited before and cut? Twenty years ago, a fellow campaigner and friend of mine was in exactly that position. When she confided in her British schoolteacher that she had been cut, her teacher's response was, 'Oh, lovely!' – she must have assumed that being cut was some kind of harmless tradition or ritual, one she knew nothing about and didn't think to question further.

In this way cultural celebrations provide a mask of acceptability, of being the norm, behind which perpetrators of an abhorrent crime can hide, and a convenient excuse for the West to avert their eyes, tiptoeing around the issue for fear of offending different cultures, of interfering or being insensitive. In my opinion, the West's reticence to date makes them co-conspirators, afraid of calling FGM what it really is – which is child abuse. But then all across the world, in different countries, they have other names for it.

In the Maasai culture, FGM is called *emuratare* and, as we've seen, usually takes place when a girl is eleven or twelve. In some Maasai tribes, in preparation for cutting, any hair on a girl's body is shaved and she is washed with cow's milk. Animals are slaughtered for a huge feast the night before, and after the cutting the girls are given animals' blood to drink in exchange for the blood they've lost. In Somalia, the *gudnin* normally takes place at a much younger age. The cutting is preceded by the gathering of family members for a feast and, as you've read in my story, the showering of gifts. In Nigeria, drummers beat their *tamas* as the girl is led towards the circumciser, who is herself decked out in juju artefacts that will help protect the girl she is cutting. And in British homes, we can only speculate, such is the secrecy of the practice in the UK – perhaps families mark this rite of passage with the same kinds of food that are eaten back in their homelands; perhaps they shower the girls with the same gifts and praise, as they talk of this 'passage into womanhood', the importance of being a 'brave girl', how 'proud' they are as parents. Research suggests that migrating communities tend to hold on to their old traditions as a way of maintaining their identity – people can find it hard to integrate or adapt, especially if they don't speak the language, and sometimes cling on to the old ways as a form of protection against the new culture in which they now find themselves.

But if you put aside these variances in custom – the traditional foods, drink, music and clothing that distinguish one FGM-practising community from the next – there is one thing that all these girls, from Maasai tribes to Manchester daughters, have in common, and that is the pain. These different rituals and rites serve only to normalise FGM within the community, and validate it as a practice in the eyes of the people who live within it. They are ceremonial smoke and mirrors that have managed to disguise the true nature of the abuse for generation after generation, so that people both inside and outside the community view the practice as an integral part of that culture's social life, intrinsic to its structure.

Without the ceremony beforehand, without the party and the presents and all the delicious foods, FGM would be laid bare for what it is – not a rite of passage, but a painful and traumatic experience forced upon a child, an entirely unnecessary mutilation that is carried out on children to satisfy the belief systems of adults. I don't doubt that the mothers and fathers of these children think that cutting them is the right thing to do – no parent would willingly harm their child if there was a choice – but the whole framing of FGM as a cultural tradition conceals the ugly truth that it is a barbaric and inhumane practice.

And of course, the nature of the area that is cut only adds to the secrecy of the abuse. If a visible part of the body was cut – an ear, an arm – would the practice then be seen differently? Instead, the pain is hidden between a woman's legs, buried deep underneath her clothes where no one needs to see it, where no one needs to be confronted by it, or be faced with the brutality of it. Everyone – the societies that practise it and those in the West who observe it – can turn their eyes away from FGM.

In 2015, a report was released by consultant paediatrician Deborah Hodes and her colleagues from the FGM children's service, based at University College London Hospitals.* It was the first

---

* 'Female genital mutilation in children presenting to a London safeguarding clinic: a case series', Deborah Hodes, Alice Armitage, Kerry Robinson and Sarah M. Creighton, *BMJ*, 18 May 2015.

paediatric literature on FGM in the developed world, and a retro-spective study of FGM cases seen by Hodes and her colleagues between 2006 and 2014. Over that time period, forty-seven girls under the age of eighteen were referred to Hodes by health profes-sionals, social workers, teachers and the police, who had suspicions that the girls had undergone FGM. There were three key findings in the report.

Firstly, there appears to be a move towards what is now being classified as Type 4 FGM. Clear evidence of cutting was found in twenty-seven of the girls: Type 1 FGM (the removal of the clitoris) was found in two girls; Type 2 (the removal of the clitoris and inner labia) was found in eight girls. No clear evidence of Type 3 (the removal of the clitoris and inner and outer labia and infibulation) was found in any of the seventeen remaining girls, although there was some evidence of adhesion or sewing together of the front of the genitals in a few cases. This might be explained, then, by an increasing prevalence of Type 4 FGM, in which the clitoris remains intact and *sunna* (pricking or nicking) takes place – the idea of *sunna* being that 'letting blood' from the clitoris lessens its 'effectiveness', and will diminish sexual desire in a woman in a similar way to removing it altogether.

The second key finding is one that chimes with the global trend of children being subjected to FGM at an ever-younger age. The majority of the girls were, like me, under the age of ten when the FGM was performed.

And the third finding is – in my opinion – the most worrying: the increased medicalisation of FGM. According to the report:

In 10 of the 27 cases (37 per cent), details of the circumstances of
FGM were not given or not known by the parent. In the remaining 17 cases, the person who performed FGM was described
as a 'doctor' in six cases (35 per cent), a 'circumciser' in seven
cases (41 per cent) ... Twelve (71 per cent) of 17 descriptions
mentioned an additional medical feature – 'anaesthetic creams',
'antibiotics', 'injections' or performed in a medical setting.

The increased medicalisation of FGM might appear at first to
be a positive development. Compared to the cutting I and others
endured without the use of any anaesthetic and in the most unhy-
gienic conditions, the thought of a girl being cut under a local or
general anaesthetic, in a sterile environment, and being properly
cared for afterwards, with the help of pain relief and antibiotics to
combat infection, is obviously appealing. When you consider that
in some communities, girls' labia are held together with thorns
and their raw and bloody flesh smeared with mud in the belief that
it has anaesthetic properties, it is not surprising that some might
welcome any kind of move towards sanitisation.

In 2001, American anthropologist Bettina Shell-Duncan wrote
a paper questioning whether the medicalisation of FGM could be
seen as 'harm reduction' or as promotion of a dangerous practice.*
In her study, she explored how 'harm reduction' had worked in the
field of AIDS, where needle-exchange programmes and education

---

* 'The Medicalization of Female "Circumcision": harm reduction or promotion of a
dangerous practice?', Bettina Shell-Duncan, Department of Anthropology, University of
Washington, 2001.

on safer drug use had been adopted in an attempt to minimise the spread of the disease. She asked whether medicalising FGM or promoting *sunna* as an alternative to more invasive forms of the practice could help save girls from a lifetime of health complications or indeed risk of death. I guess her question was: if it's going to happen anyway, could we not make sure it happens in a safe environment?

In her report she cited an initiative in both the Netherlands and the US in recent years to aid immigrants who were willing to adapt their rituals to something less invasive. The Dutch government rejected the proposal in Europe, and the so-called 'Seattle compromise', which was based on just nicking the clitoris and allowing one drop of blood to fall, was blocked by campaigners. Shell-Duncan argued that considering medicalisation as an option for communities unwilling to give up the practice should be explored, saying that if the health of women really was of paramount importance, then surely this was a worthy alternative in the interim.

But as Hodes states in her report, 'The "medicalisation" of FGM, although it reduces immediate medical risks, serves only to legitimise and prolong the practice in some communities.' In 2010, the WHO issued a report as part of a global strategy designed to stop healthcare providers from performing female genital mutilation. In it, they recognised that 18 per cent of the girls and women throughout the world who have undergone FGM had it carried out by a healthcare provider, including doctors, nurses and midwives.*

* 'Global strategy to stop health-care providers from performing female genital mutilation', WHO, 2010, p.3.

This medicalisation varied greatly, with just 1 per cent reported as medicalised cuttings in some countries, and yet 74 per cent of cuttings were carried out this way in another. The WHO condemned the practice of FGM by healthcare providers in the strongest possible terms, deeming it to be against the Hippocratic Oath.* They insisted instead that medical professionals should be educated about FGM so that they are in a position to provide support to those who have undergone it and are able to avoid being pressurised by parents to carry it out, even if they see it as harm reduction.

In the UK, in a 2004 academic study, eight young women claimed to have been cut in Britain in what they described as a hospital or clinic, although the health professionals they maintained were carrying out these procedures were clearly never identified.† Eight years later, in 2012, an undercover reporter working for the *Sunday Times* claimed to have uncovered three men in Birmingham willing to carry out FGM on her fictional daughters, aged ten and thirteen. The men – a doctor, a dentist and a practitioner of alternative medicine – first reminded the reporter that the practice was illegal, before then suggesting that she have it done abroad, and eventually agreeing, for a fee, to carry out the procedure here in this country. The tapes and transcripts of conversations were handed over to the police, but the Crown Prosecution Service decided against prosecuting the three men,

---

* 'Global strategy to stop health-care providers from performing female genital mutilation', WHO, 2010, p.16.
† 'How experiences and attitudes relating to female circumcision vary according to age on arrival in Britain: a study among young Somalis in London', Linda A. Morison, Ahmed Dirir, Sada Elmi, Jama Warsame and Shamis Dirir, 2004, p.85.

claiming that the evidence the reporter had submitted, including the statement she had for some reason refused to sign despite numerous requests, was unreliable.

FGM survivor, campaigner and former model Waris Dirie told the *Sunday Times* at the time: 'We are talking here about serious crime committed on innocent baby girls. If a white girl is abused, the police come and break the door down. If a black girl is mutilated, nobody takes care of her. This is what I call racism.' These men were willing to cut girls in this country but they were never prosecuted for this. What kind of evidence do they want? Do we wait for someone to murder a person before we prosecute them? No, we take preventative measures. It should surely make people wonder what kind of person can call themselves a doctor and yet is willing to cut pieces off children for non-medical reasons. It is worse than an ignorant village woman cutting a child, because doctors are educated, they know that a procedure like this just causes unnecessary suffering and complications for a female, and yet they are willing to do it for financial gain.

And even medicalisation of FGM doesn't ensure that girls are safe. In 1959, Egypt banned medical professionals from carrying out Type 3 FGM for fear that it legitimised the practice, but found that removing girls from clinics only forced the practice underground. As a result, in 1994 they reinstated the right of doctors in selected government hospitals to cut girls in an attempt to preserve life and lessen complications.* In 2007, however, twelve-year-old

* 'Female Genital Mutilation/Cutting: A statistical overview and exploration of the dynamics of change', UNICEF, 2013, pp.10–11.

CUT

Badour Shaker died after being circumcised at a private Egyptian clinic.* Her mother had paid just $9 for a female physician to perform the procedure on her. To buy her silence after her daughter died, the same doctor offered her $3,000. In 2008, there was an outright and blanket ban on all FGM, but six years later, the same thing happened again. Thirteen-year-old Suhair al-Bataa died after undergoing FGM at Raslan Fadl's clinic. At first the doctor denied carrying out the procedure and said she had died following an allergic reaction to penicillin. At first he was acquitted, but after an appeal he was jailed for two years for manslaughter and received three months for carrying out FGM. Suhair's father, who ordered the circumcision, was given a three-month suspended sentence. Fadl's clinic was also ordered to remain closed for one year. A pathetic penalty in exchange for this girl's life.

Even in countries where 'compromises' have been made, the practice has not been abandoned. For example, a policy in Sudan permitted the removal of the clitoris but forbade any kind of infibulation. And yet, it is believed that 88 per cent of women are still sewn up in that country.†

It seems to me that our fear of overstepping the boundaries, of offending different cultures, means that rather than pursuing a policy of zero tolerance we're instead more willing to compromise, and this should never be the case where child protection is concerned. We should adapt our principles and refuse to entertain

* http://www.theguardian.com/world/2007/jul/01/egypt.theobserver
† 'Female Genital Mutilation/Cutting: A statistical overview and exploration of the dynamics of change', UNICEF, 2013.

any form of FGM, all of our energy, efforts and initiatives should be focused on putting an end to it. In the 2013 report, 'Uncharted Territory: Violence against migrant, refugee and asylum-seeking women in Wales', it was revealed that FGM is happening to children at younger and younger ages; in fact, four out of the twenty-seven cases happened to children under the age of one.[*] The report speculates that this might be done to reduce the psychological impact, but there is nothing to say that cutting girls as babies is less psychologically damaging than when they're a bit older. In Nigeria twenty or thirty years ago it was popular to cut girls as babies. These women are only now arriving at British GPs' surgeries and antenatal clinics, and they have no idea, until they're told by a doctor or nurse, that a part of them is missing. Can you imagine the psychological impact this would have on a woman? It is hard to comprehend what these women are going through, but I'm aware that there is a lot of anger in some of those migrant communities in Britain.

The thought of FGM carried out on any child is, of course, absolutely repugnant, but to think that babies are being subjected to this unbelievable cruelty is sickening. A child's flesh is surely not even developed enough – what clitoris is there to take from a tiny baby? When I think back to taking my own babies for their jabs and soothing them as they cried, I wonder how any mother or father could stand by while their infant child, chubby legs still kicking, is mutilated to stem sexual desire. What happened to me when I was six years old

* 'Uncharted Territory: Violence against migrant, refugee and asylum-seeking women in Wales', Anne Hubbard, Joanne Payton and Dr Amanda Robinson, Wales Migration Partnership and Cardiff University, 2013.

was horrific, but at least I had a chance to know what was being done to me, at least then I could try to process it. As the report states, performing FGM on infants 'reduces the chance of the child remembering or being aware that the practice has taken place, thus reducing the chance of presentation and of a successful prosecution'.*

Consultant clinical psychologist Amanda O'Donovan works in a specialist sexual wellbeing clinic at St Bartholomew's Hospital in London, and often treats women who have been subjected to FGM. She believes that many societies have been guilty in the past of carrying out procedures on children which were seen as best for the child, but education and evolution have shown us that they were not.

'At one conference I went to, one woman said that back in the seventies, lots of kids were having their tonsils out, particularly English, middle-class kids, because it was seen as being better for children's health. So everyone went along to have their child undergo a general anaesthetic and a surgical procedure because it was *seen* to be something that was good for the child; it was culturally sanctioned. I'm not comparing the two, but it's the idea of having an understanding of why and how something happens within society.'

Is removing tonsils a necessary 'mutilation' of children's bodies? Making them go under a general anaesthetic – and all the risks that entails – purely because a mother has decided a child would be better off without their tonsils? And then you could go on:

---

* 'Female genital mutilation in children presenting to a London safeguarding clinic: a case series', Deborah Hodes, Alice Armitage, Kerry Robinson and Sarah M. Creighton, *BMJ*, 18 May 2015.

perhaps some might argue that Western women who undergo breast augmentations, or labia surgery, or piercings are, to a lesser or greater degree, mutilating themselves. People in some FGM-practising communities have even used this as a defence of their own choices – that white women in the West are allowed to trim their labia but African women aren't. And then aren't those women also doing it to fit into society's idea of what's beautiful, and specifically men's idea of what is attractive? As O'Donovan says: 'Women modify and commodify ourselves in every way – why do we wear high heels, for example?'

And yet these things have been seen as acceptable in British society – just like removing the clitoris was to some in Victorian times. It is impossible and categorically wrong to compare a child being forced to undergo FGM to a grown woman deciding to have a boob job. But is there a case to be argued that, at completely opposite ends of the scale, they represent a woman's desire or the pressures of a society on women to live up to the perception of what men want? They are females adapting themselves – or, in the case of children, females adapting one another – for the male ideal, to be more socially acceptable and therefore a more attractive prospect to men.

While we accept that FGM performed on a child is child abuse, some have contended that a grown woman has a *right* to choose whether to undergo the procedure, even if in truth that woman is only cutting herself to avoid being ostracised by her community.

But in my view, even a teenager who is considered a woman, and who seemingly goes along with her own mutilation, is not doing so because she is fully informed. She is coerced and brainwashed into thinking that it will make her a woman in the eyes of her community, her peers, her mother and her future husband. Someone being subjected to that amount of pressure cannot possibly make a choice from free will alone – whatever their age. I do agree that women everywhere are under pressure to look or behave in a certain way because they believe that's what men or the society around them wants. It is a sad admission that women's bodies are constantly being dictated to in many different ways, and all over the world.

Sunna and medicalising FGM will do nothing but collude in the subordination of women in a patriarchal society, when women around the world are fighting for rights that are equal to those of men. We can't on the one hand argue that Western women should receive equal pay with men, and then allow African or Asian women to be cut in the name of chastity. Surely equal rights mean parity among *all* women, regardless of their skin colour or the country where they were born? Culture is no excuse for the mutilation of women, nothing is. And it doesn't matter where or when or how you do it, the effects of FGM are catastrophic. There must be a zero tolerance to FGM, and this is from a woman who has been through it and knows the consequences. I didn't need to arrive in Britain to know that FGM was wrong; I knew it from when I was six years old.

17

Moving On

As with any kind of child abuse, the pain doesn't end when the act does. There are long-term physical scars that need to heal, not to mention the psychological ones. To this day I still haven't had any kind of therapy to deal with my experiences; my healing has come from sharing my story. I like to think it's worked for me, but it is also an ongoing process. It was only in the last few months, for example, as I wrote these pages, that I was able to look between my legs for the first time with a mirror. And it wasn't as frightening or horrific as it had once been, when I'd seen those photographs all those years ago. Perhaps because I'd come to terms with my story, and I'd learned to love myself and my body for all the positive things it has done, like giving birth to seven children. I realised I had more to be grateful for than angry about.

But it has taken me years to get to this stage, and many women who have gone through FGM might not have identified themselves as victims of abuse yet. It might only be when they go for their booking-in appointment with a midwife that they are asked the question about whether they have been cut, and for the first time in their lives they are offered help. It is wonderful that we can now offer women the chance to talk, especially when I think back to my own antenatal experiences. But we have to take a holistic approach to deal with survivors of FGM – it's about more than just ending the practice; it's also about supporting the women who are still suffering. In the summer of 2015, I met with doctors who are opening a specialist FGM hospital clinic in my borough, a place where women can be deinfibulated, receive counselling, perhaps even undergo reconstructive surgery if that's what they feel will help them to come to terms with their body. But as with anything, it is all dependent on funding, and the government is only just realising they have an obligation to provide the right services to help these women.

The physical side effects suffered by victims of FGM impact on them constantly. In a 2004 study of young Somalians living in London, many women talked of how their circumcision had altered their way of life, how they had even adapted themselves to walk differently for fear of breaking open their wounds.* This was always my worst fear after I was mutilated too, the terror

* 'How experiences and attitudes relating to female circumcision vary according to age on arrival in Britain: a study among young Somalis in London', Linda A. Morison, Ahmed Dirir, Sada Elmi, Jama Warsama and Shamis Dirir, 2004.

that I might come unstitched and would need to go through the agonising experience all over again – there was no more running, skipping or jumping for me, or for any of these girls, after that day.

Aside from the genital trauma, constant urinary tract infections and back pain, the list of symptoms experienced by some women after FGM goes on: kidney infections, chronic pain due to trapped or unprotected nerve endings, cysts, abscesses and genital ulcers, chronic pelvic infections, and an increase in genital infections like bacterial vaginosis. In contrast, other survivors report no ill effects as a result of their circumcision – these are the same women, however, who go on to mention in passing that it takes them fifteen minutes to urinate. I imagine these women simply have not connected the pain and discomfort they suffer as an adult to the abuse they suffered as a child, which would not be surprising if they were babies when the FGM took place and were too young to remember it.

One nurse on the front line helping women is my friend and fellow campaigner Joy Clarke. Joy has worked as a midwife at north London's Whittington Hospital for two decades; fifteen years ago she opened one of the country's first-ever dedicated FGM antenatal clinics at the hospital.

People have tiptoed around the cultural issues in the past. When I wanted to open a clinic people said, 'Why are you getting involved? It's not your culture.' I remember midwives themselves from Nigeria telling me, 'I have had it done and I'm OK.' But my responsibility has always been to the woman and the baby, to make her life better. We've come a long way, but people still question the need for an FGM clinic. But I don't care – at the end of the day I need to save lives.

Joy sees women every day who have suffered Types 1, 2 and 3 FGM. But, she says, often the problem is that the women themselves don't understand what has been done to their bodies. Dr Comfort Momoh agrees: 'What people need to realise is that some of these women have had complications all their lives, but they don't physically relate the complications to FGM. It's just something they've lived with.'

It is only in recent years that awareness of FGM has risen in the public's consciousness. Having been under the social radar for years, it has since become a much-discussed subject – this is unquestionably a positive thing, but one of the outcomes of this new focus is that suddenly survivors are under society's spotlight, and they're being told that the way they look is wrong. Research has revealed that many migrant women are anxious about seeking help once they arrive in this country for fear of being judged by medical professionals here, and I can identify with that. I was terrified to open my legs to a doctor for the first time and allow her to see what had been done to me. That's something we need to bear in mind – we must not isolate these women further. Clinical psychologist Amanda O'Donovan says she has seen some of the negative results of media campaigns labelling FGM as child abuse in British newspapers.

For some women who've come to my clinics it was the framing of it as child abuse that they found upsetting and difficult because they had made peace with their bodies. Obviously there is a political and social will to end this practice but there is a need to balance the campaign to end the practice with an understanding of the woman's individual experience, because out of a global population of millions who are being cut, not every woman will be carrying psychological damage.

Research on just how much women do suffer psychologically with the effects of FGM is still ongoing; personally, I've woken up sweating and screaming in the night from recurring nightmares my entire life. These and the flashbacks I experience in my waking day can be debilitating in themselves. I'm certainly not alone. There is evidence that women suffer unbearable psychological consequences as a result of undergoing FGM. Post-traumatic stress disorder (PTSD) is often high on the list of how women are affected. A Manchester study found that 75 per cent of women who'd suffered FGM admitted having the same recurrent and intrusive memories of the event.* In Egypt, 94.9 per cent of women reported emotional trauma of some kind.† And in 2012, a UK study by the New Step for African Community project reported the long-lasting emotional damage left by FGM on those interviewed,

---

* 'A preliminary investigation of the psychological effects of female circumcision (FGM)' (Dissertation), H. Lockhat, University of Manchester, 1999.
† 'Abusing female children by circumcision is continued in Egypt', A.A. Zayed and A.A. Ali, *Journal of Forensic and Legal Medicine*, 19 (4), 2012, pp.196–200.

particularly the difficulty they felt of suffering in silence. That's what I remember, the loneliness of suffering in a community where everyone is cut and yet no one talks about it.

A 1992 study looking at the psychosexual difficulties experienced by women who've undergone FGM found that anorgasmia (inability to orgasm) was regularly reported.* Likewise another study in 2001 found that 80 per cent of women reported 'significant sexual difficulties', with 45 per cent reporting a lack of desire for sex, 49 per cent reporting reduced pleasure and more than 60 per cent of women saying they were unable to orgasm.† Being sewn up makes sex in itself practically impossible; some healthcare workers insist that unless a woman has been opened, she cannot achieve full penetration through an infibulated vagina and a man alone cannot open her due to the rigid scar tissue. Where this is the case, it is thought that a woman gets pregnant when a man ejaculates at the opening of her vagina and the sperm swims up to her cervix.

Either way, as a practice that is primarily carried out to prevent women from having or enjoying sex, it is wholly effective. I've found it impossible to enjoy an intimate life with my husband, not only perhaps because my clitoris has been removed and is still covered, but mostly because of the psychological trauma. I can only speak for myself of course, but I have only ever associated my vagina with

---

* 'Ritual female circumcision and its effects on female sexual function', R. Brighouse, *Canadian Journal of Human Sexuality*, 1: 3–10, 1992.

† 'Female genital mutilation and its psychosexual impact', M.H. El-Defrawi, G. Lofty, K.F. Dandash, A.H. Refaat and M. Eyada, *Journal of Sex and Marital Therapy*, 27, 2001, pp.465–73.

pain and trauma. Naturally, that upsets me deeply, because how can my husband enjoy himself when he sees how much I suffer? I have been denied the basic right of a healthy sex life and I believe there are many women who feel as I do. The brutality of what took place between our legs would obviously leave its mark, and yet that doesn't stop any of us craving intimacy with the men we love. For me, it's impossible for it not to have a negative impact, although I am aware that there are plenty of FGM survivors out there who report that they do have a good sex life. Of course, one woman's experience can differ so much from another's and it's impossible for one woman to speak on behalf of all FGM survivors.

Increasingly in Britain, clinics like those run by Joy Clarke and Dr Comfort Momoh are seeing women who, like me, wish to be 'opened' before marriage. For some women, like Fatuma Farah, part of coming to terms with what has happened to them psychologically involves this physical process of deinfibulation too.

For me, the most damage FGM caused was the relationship with my mother, but at the end my mother passed away, and whatever happened between us, I forgive her. But I'm still left with myself, so something had to happen within myself and my body to end what had begun. For us FGM victims, the morning that we were cut was the beginning of something that has to end somewhere, and that ending has to come in the way it began, with a reversal operation. Something has to happen to our bodies to get closure. Of course to different women it means different things. But for me it was having the operation and convincing myself that I could make my vagina look as natural as I could. Also, for me, marrying someone from an FGM-practising community and him accepting my body for what it is was a huge part of the healing process.

Not every woman feels the same about their deinfibulation, though, and Amanda O'Donovan warns that, for some, more surgery on that area can be extremely traumatic in itself.

For many women it can be an act of reclaiming their body, but one patient who had a reversal done was actually really upset and traumatised by it. She couldn't remember her FGM, but she had images of what it might have been like and that sense of starting again with the deinfibulation was just as traumatic for her. It is not a reversal because it's not possible to return your body to the way it was when you were born. Some women feel, 'Now I'm just surgically altered in a different way,' and that's another change to process. A lot of women do feel very empowered though, having made that step, and feel like their bodies look like they do because of something they've *chosen* to do, rather than something that was done to them without their choice or consent. And, of course, when deinfibulation resolves any reproductive, gynaecological or urinary issues, that's really important for the woman's health and wellbeing.

For others, there isn't much that doctors can do, as they can't restore flesh that has been taken away. At the reversal clinic in

Tower Hamlets, she has also come across cases where reconstruction has not been clinically appropriate, and some women can experience this as another loss – they have come to the clinic hoping that it can all be undone and are told that unfortunately it can't. What Amanda is keen to stress is that any kind of deinfibulation achieves the best results when it is treated in a holistic way, addressing both the medical side and the psychological side.

Taking that next step to deinfibulate myself completely is not something that I'm willing to go through now. It's possible that I might never feel ready. For me, there is a barrier in my mind when it comes to that part of my body, and I worry that any kind of surgical procedure in that area might trigger the trauma of the cutting and the memory of the pain as I slowly healed the first time. Even today, when I have an infection down there I find it difficult because it is another thing that triggers terrible memories. To some extent, perhaps I have divorced myself from my own vagina. But perhaps it is time to finally make friends and reconnect. And there are a lot of people out there to support me, and other women like me, in starting that process.

At her clinic at St Thomas' Hospital in London, Dr Comfort Momoh carries out deinfibulations every single day. Surprisingly, in her clinical experience, 50–60 per cent of women who have had Type 3 FGM do still in fact have an intact clitoris underneath their scar tissue, so a procedure can be done to expose it, allowing the patient some sensitivity around the area during sexual intercourse. Obviously this is very positive news for survivors. There is still a relative dearth of information and research when it comes to

FGM, but Comfort's theory for why the clitoris is still present in such a significant number of cases is that it comes down to a lack of anatomical knowledge in the village circumcisers – they might not know what the clitoris or the labia actually are; they just know that they have to remove certain things from the body. Comfort has worked with communities from different countries, and she believes that in those where FGM is performed on girls as babies, there is little that is obvious to remove. Perhaps, then, what takes place is only a partial clitoridectomy, and as the baby develops, whatever is left develops too.

> I also tend to think that the circumcisers are not stupid. They have done this for many years – some might have been circumcisers for thirty or forty years. It is their job and their livelihood, and perhaps they are aware that, because of the vascularity around the area, a girl can bleed to death if you remove the clitoris. If they remove the less vascular area, which is the labia, and then cover everything together, the cutter has still satisfied the cultural needs of the procedure.

It is not just Comfort who has reported this finding. A few years ago, American gynaecological surgeon Dr Marci Bowers started working with Clitoraid, a charity that seeks to help FGM survivors all over the world to undergo reversal operations. It should be mentioned here that this charity has courted some controversy because of its links to the Raëlian religion, which backs it. Raël preaches that humans were created by extraterrestrials to enjoy untrammelled sexual pleasure, which indeed does raise some eyebrows, and yet there is no doubt that the cause they've taken up helping FGM survivors is a noble one, so it's worth hearing what they have to say. Dr Bowers is keen to point out that she is not a 'Raëlian' but a doctor, and since her training was sponsored by the organisation she has performed reconstructive surgery on 150 patients, many of whom had travelled from Britain to her clinic in California for help, for which she does not charge. Like Comfort, Dr Bowers has noted that a full reconstruction isn't always necessary – one in five of the women she sees has a clitoris that is completely intact. 'The cutters are not trying to injure the girl, they are doing it as a rite of passage. These are often their loved ones, their friends' children, their nieces. They are doing it to control sexuality, and they know not to go very deep and put the girl's life in danger.'

Dr Bowers gained her expertise from training with the pioneering and well-respected French urological surgeon Pierre Foldès, who developed a technique that would help reconstruct victims of FGM. Like many doctors, before she joined Clitoraid, Dr Bowers had very little understanding of what FGM is, and was sceptical about the possibility of clitoral reconstruction, in part due to having only a superficial knowledge of the nature of the clitoris.

FGM is not as destructive medically as you first think because what it does more than anything is obscure the clitoris by burying it under scar tissue. There is a lot of clitoris, it isn't a 2mm piece of tissue, it's much larger – just as in males, where the erogenic area of the pelvis when mapped out is much larger than

231

advertised, so the clitoris is literally the tip of the iceberg. There is an 8 per cent mortality rate overall from FGM – the cutters know only to go very superficially, mainly removing the labia minora and the clitoral hood, and not to go too deeply into the clitoral body. The clitoral body is where most of the sensation is from, so the reversal process means we're trying to locate that clitoral body and bring it to the surface. You just need to dig beneath the surface and it's always there, one hundred per cent of the time.

Prior to talking with Dr Bowers I'd had no idea just what a huge and deep organ the clitoris is. 'It just goes to show that such superficial attention is paid to a woman's sexuality,' she says. 'Socially and globally, people just don't talk about it. This is due to vestiges of past Victorian attitudes which are dismissive of women's sexuality, but if you understand that area of the body then you realise that there is so much more to it. We shouldn't be so afraid of it.' Dr Bowers admits that reconstructing the labia isn't always possible – once skin is gone, after all, it's gone. For her, finding the clitoris is, in her words, 'the money spot'. However, while surgery offers so much hope to women, she's also very mindful of the trauma it can cause too, and acknowledges that the reactions of patients vary from individual to individual.

Women don't usually come forward because they want any kind of restoration of pleasure; they come forward because they feel their identity was stolen by FGM. They want to reclaim their identity, and many psychological effects can be gained by doing that – they receive validation for what they went through; it can be an opportunity to connect with other women who have gone through it; they can often feel more engaged sexually after surgery. But women can find it difficult too; they can be surprised by the sensations that they are left with because the clitoris is fairly unprotected and they can be surprised by how sensitive that area is. Mostly that can be a good thing, especially if prior sensations in that area were associated with negative feelings. It's very complicated because there is also a risk of re-traumatising women.

It's important, therefore, that women also have psychological support when they go through any kind of reconstruction; although Dr Bowers offers her surgical skills for free, and a number of psychotherapists have offered their time to her team, it can still be harder to secure as much voluntary psychological assistance as she would like. Nevertheless, the fact that this service is free is an acknowledgement of how important this issue is worldwide. 'We don't charge patients because Pierre Foldès did not charge for his work,' says Dr Bowers. 'He feels FGM is a crime against humanity so therefore it would be unethical to charge for reconstructions. In my work I'm able to pay my bills through other means. It's a beautiful thing to be a part of.'

Thirty-eight-year-old Pamela Okah-Bischof from Nigeria is one of those women living in Britain who has sought reconstructive work. She says that undergoing this surgery was, for her, a way of resolving the anger she felt at the fact that she had been subjected to Type 1 FGM when she was a young girl.

I remember clearly what happened to me. I was eight or nine at the time. I had been sleeping that morning in my brother's room because I had watched a movie that was scary the night before and I didn't want to sleep alone. Between 5:30 and 6am, my father and stepmother came to get me out of my brother's room. My father told me I was going to do what my sisters had done and I was going on my journey towards being a woman. I said to him, 'What does it mean to be a woman?' and he said, 'Don't worry.' There were two hefty women there and one small-ish one, and she carried the little bag with her. They asked me to go into my room and already there was a mat on the floor. They asked me to take off my bottoms and lie down, and just as I hit the floor the two women jumped me. One of them sat on my chest and held my arms down, the other two tore at my legs . . .

I didn't think anything about FGM as I was growing up. At first, when it happened, I didn't think about culture or anything like that. For me at that time FGM was not a crime; it was just something they had to do to you. It was later on when I started having the flashbacks, and when I came to the UK and I started to research it, that I had a lot of anger issues. I didn't care that it was a traditional or cultural thing – my father was a very edu-cated man and I didn't expect that he would have gone down this route. For me there was a lot of anger, but my father passed away so I never had the opportunity to speak to him about it.

Pamela's way of dealing with the anger was to take back control of her own body by searching for help. She attended Comfort's clinic, where they cut open the scar tissue over her clitoris in order to expose it. But this, for Pamela, was not enough of a reversal. She felt something had been taken away from her and that perhaps someone could give it back. It wasn't about her sex life – she had always been able to orgasm – but about her psychological wellbeing. As a midwife, she sees vaginas on a daily basis, and she wanted to be able to look at herself and feel that she also had a normal vagina. 'If I didn't know what normal was it wouldn't have been an issue for me, but for me it was done at an age when I remember so many things and I can't forget what happened. It was the fact that I knew something had happened that was killing me more than anything else.'

At first, Pamela travelled to Paris for surgery. When they were unable to reconstruct the clitoral hood, which she dearly wanted, she contacted the Desert Flower Foundation in Berlin. There, a plastic surgeon was able to give her the vagina she wanted.

Women think that it's traumatic to have surgery, but ... when you wake up you feel like a different person. You wake up knowing that something has changed. The experience psychologically for me was completely different. When they carry out FGM, they don't put you to sleep; you don't have people around you, talking to you, or counsellors like they had in Berlin. [When you're having the reconstructive surgery] nobody is pinning you down or cutting you against your will – this is someone trying to help you. You tell them what you want and they do what you ask. I had complete control over the situation. It is very empowering, and there wasn't any pain when I woke up.

Pamela had her surgery in July 2015, and she has now set up the Revive Foundation, which aims to fund women travelling to Berlin for reconstructive surgery. She is a strong advocate of women following their hearts, and pursuing reconstructive surgery if they feel that it will help them come to terms with their circumcision. 'It hasn't given me complete closure. I don't think you can ever get closure because mentally you know that you've been touched. You still get that flash of anger once in a while. You will always regret that you were made a victim of your parents. But it's one more step, for me, towards reconciliation with my father, my stepmother and with myself.'

Aside from the potential psychological benefits of deinfibulation, there is often a very practical need for the procedure. Joy Clarke remembers the first time she came across FGM in her clinical career as a midwife, twenty years ago. A woman turned up on Joy's ward in the very last stages of labour, having suffered Type 3 FGM. As mentioned, some women fall pregnant without ever having been deinfibulated. Joy's patient, a dentist from Sudan, was already fully dilated when she arrived. 'The reason we knew this was because, through the tiny hole that remained of her vagina, the baby's long black hair was twisting and turning.' The baby was there, waiting to be delivered, but it couldn't get out because the woman was still entirely infibulated. The woman was obviously in great distress, and she was not alone.

The woman was yelling, and you want to be calm and to be able to console her, but everyone was panicking. The room was full of doctors and midwives, and I was so shocked, my back was against the wall. The doctor was frightened, the woman was frightened, and the doctor had no choice but to do an anterior episiotomy – that is, he cut her up the front, upwards of her vagina – and the second he did, the baby just fell out. The baby had been pushing against a closed door, and the minute it was open, it fell out on to the bed.

It is impossible to imagine the fear that woman must have felt as she tried to give birth to her baby, and this is why clinics like Joy's and Comfort's aim to identify women before they get to that stage of pregnancy. If that doctor hadn't opened the woman there and then, both her life and the baby's might have been lost. Imagine a similar scenario taking place out in rural communities – it's no wonder that FGM is linked to both maternal and infant death. Today, the procedure at many antenatal clinics is to identify FGM survivors early on in their pregnancy, so they can be opened between twenty and thirty-two weeks, allowing time for them to heal before the birth. Of course, pregnancy should be a time of happiness, when a woman enjoys the way her body changes and grows as she feels the baby kick inside her, rather than a process that involves undergoing yet more surgery and potentially reliving the initial trauma in the recovery period following the deinfibulation. But at least a partial deinfibulation, like I had, is a necessary thing to do, even if the woman hasn't had a full Type 3 cutting. If her urethra is covered by scar tissue, this could cause huge complications in an emergency situation, particularly if she needed to undergo a Caesarean and had to be catheterised.

A 2006 WHO study of more than 28,000 women in obstetric centres across various African countries found that women who had undergone FGM were much more likely to experience serious complications during their labour.* The report found that those who had been subjected to Type 3 FGM were 30 per cent more likely to require a Caesarean than women who hadn't had any form of FGM. There was also a 70 per cent increase in the number of women with Type 3 experiencing postpartum haemorrhages. Babies born to mothers with Type 3 FGM also had an 86 per cent higher chance of requiring resuscitation. The death rate among babies during and immediately after birth was also worryingly higher for mothers with FGM – 15 per cent higher in those with Type 1, 32 per cent higher in those with Type 2, and 55 per cent higher in those with Type 3. I'm quite sure that had antenatal care of the kind offered by Joy and Comfort been available to women in these African countries, such desperately sad cases could have been prevented. Babies born in Britain to FGM survivors will be much safer, but any increased risk is always of concern. Of course, no woman knows what she will face when going into labour, but the statistics of how FGM survivors – and their babies – suffer speak for themselves.

Why this tradition, favoured by generations past, would continue today in the knowledge that it puts future generations at risk is just incomprehensible to me – or perhaps they simply haven't read the same information as we have. If they don't have access to

---

* 'Female genital mutilation and obstetric outcome', WHO study group, 2006.

all the facts, how will they ever know? It helps to understand the conflicting messages mothers receive, passed down from generation to generation – messages from men, from society, from their peers. I believe the more we strive to understand the context of these women's actions, the closer we will be to helping mothers – both abroad and in the UK – make an alternative choice, like many others already have. Joy Clarke has had many women confide to her that they, like me, asked to be cut – as if in some way this means they were responsible for what happened to them, when clearly they were coerced or subtly pressured into it, if not by their parents, then by the wider community. Just like the one I heard in the playground, the message from those societies is: be cut and then you will be part of this community.

Ten years ago, a young girl, very close to me, was taken to Tanzania to be cut in the school holidays. Laila had come to this country from Somalia when she was three and had thrived in Britain – she was a bright, outgoing and happy young woman. She was an excellent student and had just sat her GCSE exams, scoring As and Bs across the board, and was due to take up a place in college after the summer break to study chemistry. She remembered nothing of Somalia; Britain was the only home she knew. I had no idea her mother planned to take her away and have her cut until I received a phone call from Tanzania. I begged her mother not to cut Laila, and urged her not to make the same mistake that our mothers had. But her mind was made up; she was adamant and I was thousands of miles away unable to help. Back then I'd heard stories about women taking girls over to places like Tanzania and

Dubai in the holidays, how many families paid $200 for a Type 2 procedure under a general anaesthetic in a hospital. Nothing about the sanitised conditions made me feel any better about it.

The girl who came home from Tanzania was different to the one who'd left six weeks earlier. She was angry, at loggerheads with her mother – and remains so to this day, ten years on. Of course I can see why, but she insists to me that it wasn't being cut that changed her. Laila has told me: 'It's OK, I'm not in any pain. I don't feel anything. It's not a big deal.' I know from my own experience that this is unlikely to be the case, and I can see for myself how much it has changed her. Laila told me that she didn't want to be cut, but there had been five or six family members – all women – who had coerced her into it. They told her it was a good thing, that it would make her mother happy – who was she to refuse when so many of her cousins seemed convinced that FGM was the right path to choose? And so she said yes, and it destroyed her. She was brainwashed. The girl I knew before was high-achieving; she had great goals and a whole life ahead of her. The girl I know now drifts from job to job; she doesn't know what she wants. All she feels is an anger burning deep inside of her.

I knew that her mother had broken the law by taking her, but I didn't have the courage to speak out at the time. If it had happened now, I would move mountains to stop that girl from being cut. But back then I was only just discovering that what had happened to me was child abuse; I certainly wasn't ready or able to accept that it was happening to others. Today I can see that Laila is still not ready to talk about FGM, but she knows I'll be here to listen when she is. She is just another example of the girls who are trapped between two cultures, the ones who straddle the void between what their parents want and what they want as a child or teenager growing up in Britain. Can you imagine the pressure that she was put under to agree to be mutilated and the number of lies that she was told to get her to agree? And these lies came from people she knew and trusted.

This is not a story that is unfamiliar to Dr Comfort Momoh. She sees plenty of women in her London clinic who were taken and cut against their will by parents who wanted to abide by old traditions, and yet wanted their children to be able to have all the very best that a life in the West could afford them.

'We need to empower the young people,' she says. 'Young people will say, "I have to follow my culture", but they get trapped between two cultures – they want to satisfy their parents' needs but at the same time they want to belong to the West's community and culture.'

So many girls must fall into this trap, the space between two cultures, of naturally feeling loyalty towards their family, and yet holding dear the British values that they've been brought up with. All children want to please their parents; none of them want to cause disappointment or upset. And yet what is being done to them is totally at odds with Western values, where they may have learned in schools that FGM is wrong. In Britain, we might bring our daughters up to value their bodies, to not become intimate with someone until they are really sure about them. Guidance and information about relationships and sex are gained from within the family; we want our children to be safe. What we don't do is sew them up from top to bottom to make absolutely sure that they save themselves for their future husbands.

A 2013 UNICEF report revealed that social acceptance is still the most frequently cited reason for supporting the practice of FGM.* I can well believe it because I saw it for myself. I wanted to be accepted by my friends, so I asked my mother to cut me. Therefore, I was complicit in my own abuse, just like so many of the other girls I played with, although none of us would have realised that at the time. But it is impossible at four, six, or even sixteen, to know just what FGM is and how it will affect your life. 'It's just a little cut,' they tell you. I often thought about that as I lay recovering from the butchering I received at my own request. Just like most children, we thought we knew everything. We talked about these adult words and phrases as if they meant the same to us as they did to our parents, and yet we had no idea what we were in for.

In FGM-practising communities, society and family tell girls that it is shameful not to be cut, that's the lie they spin, or rather that's the myth they themselves believe. As well as the fact that it's portrayed as only a tiny cut, you are told that you are 'brave' if you are cut, that you are not 'dirty', that it will make you a 'good girl', a 'big girl'– who doesn't want to hear those things as a child? Who wants to be labelled as an unclean coward? Being cut seems like a small price to pay compared to being called that. One FGM survivor explained to the authors of the report, 'Uncharted Territory: Violence against migrant, refugee and asylum-seeking women in Wales': 'Growing up, no one says it's wrong. At school there was a perception that you are not a woman unless you

* 'Female Genital Mutilation/Cutting: A statistical overview and exploration of the dynamics of change', UNICEF, 2013.

have been circumcised. Now I am in Wales, I can see it's wrong.'*

A further aspect of this debate to consider is the women who are forced into work as cutters. A few years ago, the Home Office heard an asylum application from a woman from Sierra Leone, who had inherited the mantle of cutter in the Bondo society. These women-only societies wield great power in Sierra Leone, and cutters are held in very high esteem within their community, which is why their powers are handed down through generations. Here, the women are not cut for men, but as a form of initiation into these societies of women which hold significant political sway. Except this woman didn't want it, and she knew she wouldn't be able to continue to survive in that society if she didn't take over the role, which would also put her own daughters at risk. It was a dilemma that, had she stayed within her community, would have affected her psychologically and, perhaps, physically. What penalties would she have faced for going against her community and tradition? She probably knew that it was not an option she could consider, and so she applied for asylum to this country on the basis that she had the right not to be coerced into becoming a cutter and therefore a perpetrator of FGM. The Supreme Court accepted her argument in principle, yet rejected her claim on the basis that she came from a rural area in Sierra Leone, so she would be able to live peacefully in the capital, Freetown. We can only hope that she did, rather than succumb to the pressure to comply with this age-old custom that she seemed to determined to escape.

* 'Uncharted Territory: Violence against migrant, refugee and asylum-seeking women in Wales', Anne Hubbard, Joanne Payton and Dr Amanda Robinson, Wales Migration Partnership and Cardiff University, 2013.

This woman is an example of the next generation desperate to move away from a life they would otherwise have been expected to continue. It is another example of how attitudes are changing between generations, but it feels like frustratingly slow progress. One thing that does seem to speed up the process is migration. A 2004 academic report found that the younger girls and boys are when they come to live in Britain, the more likely they are to abandon these traditions.* The authors of the report interviewed 200 single male and female Somalians between the ages of sixteen and twenty-two living in Greater London. They found that those who were living in Britain before the age of six (the usual time a girl would be circumcised) were less likely to be circumcised (42 per cent) than those who arrived after the usual age for circumcision (91 per cent). So we could assume that for many, although sadly not all, coming to Britain itself seems a huge reason to abandon the practice. But of course this is dictated by the parents. What of the children, though – how does it affect how they think and feel about FGM?

In 2013 a report by UNICEF – 'Female Genital Mutilation/Cutting: A statistical overview and exploration of the dynamics of change' – revealed some interesting data about the difference between how girls aged fifteen to nineteen viewed the practice as opposed to women aged forty-five to forty-nine.† In my country,

---

* 'How experiences and attitudes relating to female circumcision vary according to age on arrival in Britain: a study among young Somalis in London', Linda A. Morison, Ahmed Dirir, Sada Elmi, Jama Warsame and Shamis Dirir, 2004.
† 'Female Genital Mutilation/Cutting: A statistical overview and exploration of the dynamics of change', UNICEF, 2013.

Somalia, for example, 64 per cent of women were in favour of FGM continuing, and 60 per cent of girls. However, in Egypt, the difference of opinion was much greater, with 64 per cent of women being in favour of FGM, as opposed to 34 per cent of girls. In the majority of cases, support for FGM is a lot stronger in the older group of women, and yet in Uganda just 4 per cent of women think the practice should continue and 13 per cent of girls. However, and overwhelmingly, all the evidence seems to indicate that, with each generation that passes, support lessens, which is exactly what we want to hear, and more education on the subject will only decrease the number of supporters in both age ranges.

I know myself that education plays a huge part in the abandonment of FGM. Many surveys have revealed that girls who are in secondary education are less likely to be cut and more likely to want the practice abolished. In the 2013 UNICEF report, for example, girls and women in Sudan who have had no formal education are nearly four times more likely to support FGM than girls and women with secondary or higher education. Perhaps unsurprisingly, more than 60 per cent of Somalian girls who have received a Koranic education support FGM, compared to almost 50 per cent of those who've received a secondary education – despite the fact that it is not a religious practice.

What of the attitudes of migrants living in Britain, or British girls whose parents were born in practising countries? Can their migration, or that of their parents, be enough to turn them away from FGM? Personally, I don't believe that migration itself is enough. For example, in some cultures, migration has proved to be a *reason* to continue the practice as a way of identifying and re-establishing tribes once they have settled into new countries they plan to call home. Nor do I believe that the law alone is enough to turn people away from this barbaric practice. The most effective way to change attitudes is through education, and not just of children born into migrant communities, but all British children. I'm amazed, when I give talks in secondary schools, just how few hands go up when I ask who has heard of FGM. If white British teenage girls don't know what FGM is, how can they help their friends who might be at risk?

That is exactly what Muna Hassan has found. Muna is a twenty-one-year-old FGM campaigner from Bristol. Her Somalian parents came over to Britain when she was three, although Muna was actually born in Sweden. She and her friends co-founded Integrate Bristol four years ago along with teacher, Lisa Zimmerman. The charity was aimed at promoting gender equality among migrant communities, but they quickly made FGM one of their top priorities. Muna is a great example of the changing attitudes of British girls with regard to FGM today. When I spoke to her, she told me she had seen a huge shift in thinking since her campaigning began a few years ago. 'Attitudes towards FGM have changed so much within the last couple of years. The things I was seeing when I was sixteen and things I'm hearing now are worlds apart,' she says. Muna started Integrate Bristol with three other girls. When FGM came up in discussion, Muna had never heard of it, even though both her parents are from Somalia. She and her co-campaigners were talking about violence towards women and girls, about rape, forced marriage, child marriage, and when someone mentioned FGM, Muna assumed it was something to do with the economy, or a bank. She was horrified when she later Googled the term and discovered that 98 per cent of Somalian girls are cut. She then came across the word *gudnin* and realised that over the years she had heard it mentioned in her own community – she just hadn't known what it was.

At first it was very shameful to talk about and no one considered it to be an issue, not just in the community – even the staff in our school didn't think it was a problem. They just saw it as a cultural practice; it wasn't abuse to them. People genuinely felt uncomfortable discussing it, because all of a sudden you're challenging something that's been going on for centuries in our culture, and also remember that some of the girls I was discussing it with had gone through it themselves ... Suddenly we were saying everything that happened to you is wrong. It's already hard enough being a teenager, you're going through so many different emotions and experiencing so many different things, and then you have this added on top.

We were really naive as young people, so I couldn't blame the girls at school who had gone through it for being angry at me. I wasn't just challenging her – I was challenging something that her family had let happen to her, something that had happened to her body. It wasn't about saying your body is wrong and this is how it's supposed to be; it was about empowering her and asking, would you do this to your child? It was about the future.

247

It didn't mean that Muna didn't face opposition. Some in the Somalian community in Bristol were outraged that she was discussing something so private – particularly when she and fellow campaigners decided to make a short drama about FGM, *Silent Scream*. The pressure from some in the community became very intense, to the point where Muna felt it was almost bullying. Rumours were spread by her peers at school about her and her co-campaigners – that they were taking drugs, that they were making a porn film, that they were showing their private parts on film – in an attempt to spur their parents into action, to demand that Muna pull out of the campaigning work. Muna also told me that 'some men in the Somali community were really angry about it too.'

However, it was the positive reaction of Somalian mothers within the community that surprised and delighted Muna and her friends most of all. 'All the mothers had to sign a permission slip before we could join the campaigning and their way of protesting and being really angry about what the men were doing was by signing those permission slips. I think for me that was the most empowering thing to see – your mum knows exactly what you are doing and she's willing to stand up for you.'

It's incredible to me to hear Muna's story, because that group of four girls soon swelled to a campaigning cohort, made up of both boys and girls, of eighty-six within her school. Most importantly, their work was changing the opinions of their own parents, and making them think twice about FGM. Not that Muna needed to worry about that with her parents, but she was anxious about their reaction initially, and what they'd think in terms of a community backlash, but she received incredible support from both her mother and father. 'My dad was so happy and so proud of me; he told me so much needed changing. And I thought to myself, if we can normalise this, if I can even speak to my parents about it, it's not a hidden abuse anymore. That's what we used to call it, the silent abuse, but it isn't like that anymore ... The likelihood of a girl going through FGM in this country is very high, and to say it doesn't happen in the UK is us just lying to ourselves.'

Muna admits that it is hard to monitor change – she doesn't know for sure if FGM will stop in her community as a result of her hard work. Stories such as hers feel like such a positive step forward compared to the girls I was at school with. Yes, these children are talking about FGM, but in a completely different way to when I was at school. All the young people in Muna's school have now had peer sessions on FGM, and all the staff have been trained. People are no longer so uncomfortable when it comes to discussing the subject. 'It's really inspiring to see girls who have gone through the practice before they came to the country saying: "Yeah, I've gone through this. I can accept what's happened to me." And everyone in a room accepts it too. They say, "This has happened, but we can all move on together."'

As Muna says, it's about the future. However much we like to pretend or how much we claim it to be a cultural practice – and yes it is – it is still child abuse. Muna herself has noticed a shift, now, in the terminology that people use when they're talking about FGM. 'Just watching those young people be empowered enough to say, "No, I'm never going to let this happen to my daughter", is enough. That's when you know you've made a change.'

Epilogue

A few weeks ago I was sitting on the 257 bus, on my way home
from work. It was late afternoon and, as autumn made its
descent into winter, the sky was darkening deep blue earlier and
earlier. People around me bustled on to the bus, bringing with
them a rush of cold air and the odd rusty leaf that had stowed
away with them on to the red double-decker, and then, through
the crowds of people standing up, I spotted a woman heading
towards me. She was wearing a full black *abaya* and a black *niqab*
on her head; even her hands were hidden away in gloves, and just
her eyes were visible. She was Somalian, clearly deeply religious
judging by the way she was dressed, and she sat down beside me.

'You are Hibo Wardere,' she said. It wasn't easy to read her
expression, and I searched her eyes for a clue to what was going
on in her thoughts, but they seemed cold and angry.

'Yes,' I said.

'You did a talk at my daughter's school. You told her about FGM, you told her everything about it!'

I looked down and saw that her gloved hands were gesticulating wildly. She was clearly really cross, and perhaps I would have felt a little anxious if I wasn't on a crowded bus, and yet curiosity got the better of me – I wanted to know what her daughter had told her to make her so angry.

'What did your daughter tell you?' I asked.

'She said that you told her that FGM is wrong, that it is child abuse, that if she is in trouble she should call 999 or tell a teacher.'

I smiled. 'What else did she tell you?'

'You told her that I could go to jail for fourteen years if she is cut. You told her about the medical problems. You told her she has human rights.'

She was getting angrier and angrier.

'How dare you go into my daughter's school and talk to her about these things!'

I looked at her then, trying so hard to wipe the smile from my face, but I wasn't worried by what she was telling me. I was excited, because I'd done my job; I'd educated her daughter and then she'd gone home and educated her mother. She'd told her everything exactly as I'd said it. I had to keep the pride from bubbling over in my voice as I spoke.

'You're obviously a religious person,' I said to her, lowering my voice to just above a whisper. 'Do you think you are bigger than God?'

Her eyes widened. 'No!' she said.

'So why do you think that He created your daughter imperfect? Why do you feel the need to change her body?'

Her eyes flashed furious then. She started ranting at me and, as she did, the bus driver had heard enough. He left his cabin and came to the back of the bus, then he opened the doors and told her to get off.

'Me?' she said.

He nodded. Then, when she'd left, he thanked me for not raising my voice back at her. But I didn't need thanks, because that woman had given me the greatest gift she ever could and she didn't even know it. That woman had taught me just how worthwhile my work was, just how much it was working. I needed no further proof than my words that she'd repeated back to me through her daughter. My message was getting through.

There is an old Somalian proverb which says: 'You can't hide a dead body from its grave'. Its meaning? You can't hide from your problems. Abuse thrives in secrecy, whereas out in the open it wilts and dies. The more we can bring abuse of any kind out into the world, where we can examine it and talk about it, the more likely we are to see the back of it. FGM is nothing more than child abuse. You can dress it up in whatever cultural clothing you want, but it is that basic. It is wrong to take a child against her will and mutilate her for the sake of preserving her for a man. It is wrong to risk her life to save a tradition. It is wrong to condemn her to a lifetime of pain and suffering, to the possibility of infertility or a higher risk of death in childbirth.

FGM is wrong.

You can't hide a body from its grave.

Once we all know about female genital mutilation, none of us can carry on pretending it isn't our problem.

Acknowledgements

First I want to thank my children. They gave me the second chance to live the moments that I lost in my own childhood: they are my strength, my love and give me the will to fight to go on every day. This book is dedicated to them.

I'd also like to thank everyone who made this book possible: Anna Wharton for her collaboration; Abigail Bergstrom, Jo Whitford and everyone at my publisher Simon & Schuster; Robyn Drury and the team at Diane Banks Associates.

Thank you to the people who gave their time and expertise to talk to me and Anna for this book: Fatuma Farah, Abbas, Mohamed, Dr Comfort Momoh, Solomon Zewolde, the London Metropolitan Police, Zimran Samuel, Dexter Dias QC, Deborah Hodes, Amanda O'Donovan, Joy Clarke, Dr Marci Bowers, Pamela Okah-Bischof, Muna Hassan, Lisa Zimmerman, Hannah Weaver of Cricket Without Boundaries, Louise Robertson of 28 Too Many, Agnes Pareyio of the Tasaru Ntomonok Initiative, Nadine Gary and Brendan Wynne of Equality Now.

And thank you to the friends, colleagues and family members who have supported me and my work over the years, and to the amazing children I teach about FGM, who are so inspiring to me.